AN iPHONE GUIDE
FOR GRANDPARENTS

LEARNING FROM A MEM▮▮▮▮▮▮▮▮ GREW
UP ON THE INTERNE▮▮▮▮▮▮▮ MEDIA

FIRST EDITION

CARTER KOWALSKI

ISBN: 9798697879283

AN *iphone* GUIDE FOR GRANDPARENTS

LEARNING FROM A MEMBER OF iGEN, WHO GREW UP ON THE INTERNET AND SOCIAL MEDIA

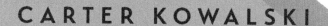

CARTER KOWALSKI

DEDICATION

For my Mimi and Bampa.
Thank you for always encouraging me to
be the best version of myself.

TABLE OF CONTENTS

CHAPTER ONE

INTRODUCTION

So you have a new iPhone. A little daunting, I know, but I can promise you that you will soon be a pro! It can be a little scary at first, but I have complete confidence in you and your abilities.

And so it sits on the table in front of you. A little rectangular piece of metal. There is so much that you can do with it, and so many different ways of doing the same thing.

Before we get into how to operate your new piece of technology, let me explain who I am, and why I am able to teach you about your new phone. Hi. My name is Carter, and I am seventeen. The idea to write this book came to me when I was teaching my Grandmother about her new iPhone. I realized that there are probably other people out there that would like help too.

And so, I sat down, and started brainstorming ideas about what to write about, how I should structure the book, and what types of things I should talk about.

But the longer I thought about it, the more I realized that learning something new, especially something that can be confusing, should be natural. And so, throughout this book, I will be teaching you how to use your phone as if I am one of your grandkids (if you don't have any grandkids, congratulations you have me now).

Before we start, I would like to share a little story with you. When I first found out that my grandmother got an iPhone, she surprised me, and FaceTimed me. I was in complete shock, looking at my phone, and seeing her name as the caller ID. When I answered the call, we began talking and catching up. She lives on the other side of the country, so I don't see her that often, but we like to text and FaceTime each other.

When we were talking about her buying her iPhone and the process that she went though, she told me about the worker that sold her the phone. The worker was kind enough to help her through the set-up process of the phone, and explain a couple of the basic functions. The worker told my grandmother that a lot of other people her age would typically come back to the store a couple of days later, frustrated because they couldn't figure out how to work their new phone. It isn't easy. And so, this worker challenged my grandmother to explore her phone as much as she possibly could, and learn as much as she could, without anyone's help. Within a couple of days, my grandmother was able to work her phone pretty fluently. She had done it.

This is what I am challenging you to do. After you read this book, you will know so much about your iPhone. But I cannot possibly teach you everything there is to know about it. After you finish this book, I challenge you to explore your phone for yourself.

While talking with my grandma during that same FaceTime call, she had said something to me that really stuck with me; "There is nothing that you can or can not do. You can do anything you want to do, you just have to believe that you can". I think that this is 100% true when it comes to learning about your new phone. I believe that you can do this, and I want you to believe in yourself too. Try to keep an open and relaxed mind while learning about your phone; it'll make the process more enjoyable and you will learn and remember so much more!

And so, I sit at the table writing this book. I have my iPhone in my hand, you have yours in your hand. I will be going through the movements and gestures with you, as we control our phones together.

CHAPTER TWO

CATEGORIZATION OF YOUR iPHONE

Before we get into learning about features, gestures, and learning other things about your phone, I have to teach you three concepts that will help you understand what model your phone is, and why this changes some of the things that you can or can't do on your phone.

THERE ARE MANY DIFFERENT TYPES OF PHONES

This one might be daunting to hear. There are many different types of phones, and each one has different features and functions. This book is solely angled toward iPhones; so that helps us narrow it down a little bit.

The word "phone" is an umbrella, or general, term for the device in which you can call, text, etc. There are different types of phones; mainly smartphones and non-smartphones. Smartphones are phones that are able to connect to the internet (like LTE) as well as being able to call or text. Non-smartphones are typically just used for calling and texting. All iPhones are smartphones, meaning that you can call, text, access the internet, and do a ton of other things all on the same device.

However, there are different types of iPhones. Typically, newer models of iPhones are released each year, with new features that make them better or faster than the previous models. Here is a list of all the iPhones that are currently released:

iPhone (2007)

iPhone 3G

iPhone 3GS

iPhone 4

iPhone 4S

iPhone 5

iPhone 5c

iPhone 5s

iPhone 6

iPhone 6 Plus

iPhone 6s

iPhone 6s Plus

iPhone SE (2016)

iPhone 7

iPhone 7 Plus

iPhone 8

iPhone 8 Plus

iPhone X

iPhone XR

iPhone XS

iPhone XS Max

iPhone 11

iPhone 11 Pro

iPhone 11 Pro Max

iPhone SE (2020)

Here is a list of all the iPhones released in chronological order, from oldest to newest. This book was written in early 2020, so if you are reading this book after this date, then there will be additional iPhones on the list. You can look up a current list if you are curious to see if there are any newer devices that out there.

Regardless of the device that you have (or are going to buy), they are all fantastic devices, and will work beautifully for you.

If you haven't bought your iPhone yet, there will be a buying guide in the next chapter that will help you narrow down your decision. However, if you already have you device, then you will have to identify which device you have.

To identify what model your device is, you there are a couple of different places you can check. First, I'd say check the box that your phone came in. It will usually say it on the side of the box or on the back. You can also check the back of the phone itself (some models have it engraved right on the back).

OPERATING SYSTEMS

In addition to a new iPhone (or iPhones) being released each year, new operating systems for these phones (also known as iOS) are released. Users can download new operating systems whenever they are released for free.

These "updates", as they are called, update your current operating system to the newer one. Typically, they are announced by Apple in June or July, and users are able to download them in September, October, or November (these dates could be different in the future, but in the past, they have typically been in these months).

Experts agree that you should update your device when they are available, because they have added security features, and add other features that can make the experience of using your phone more enjoyable. You don't have to update it though, and I'd say that you can just ignore software updates, unless you really want to have the benefits of a new iOS. We will learn how to update your iPhone in the future if you would like to do so.

TOUCH ID VS. FACE ID

Another differentiating factor between these iPhones, is that some of them have Touch ID, and some of them have Face ID. There isn't a major difference between Face ID and Touch ID; they are just different ways of unlocking your iPhone.

If your device is an iPhone 5s - iPhone 8 Plus (on that list), then your phone has Touch ID. This is also indicated by the circular home button just below the screen.

If you have an iPhone X - iPhone 11 Pro Max (according to the list on the previous page), then you have Face ID. This is also indicated by the fact that you do not have a home button below the screen. It is also indicated by the fact that your phone has a notch at the top of the display (see the pictures below).

The iPhone SE 2020 (at the bottom of the list), is unique, in the way that it doesn't follow the general trend of newer phones having Face ID. The iPhone SE 2020 has a circular home button below the screen, and therefore uses Touch ID to unlock the phone.

Note: This circular button, is also known as the "home button".

The 2007 iPhone - iPhone 5s do not have Face ID or Touch ID, and therefore the user is just prompted to enter the phone's passcode. You don't have to worry about this if you do not have one of those devices, as they are relatively old at this point and very few people have them.

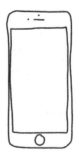

This phone has Face ID. It does not have a circular button on the bottom. It also has a notch on the top of the display.

This phone does have a circular button below the screen. Therefore it has Touch ID.

That was a lot of information, I know. I apologize for slamming you with a lot of technical information before we even learn how to use your iPhone! Knowing what category your phone falls into will be helpful later.

Are you ready to get started? I sure am, and I know that you are too! Don't be scared or anxious. I promise that <u>you</u> will become a pro, and using your new phone will be natural.

CHAPTER THREE

HAVEN'T BOUGHT YOUR PHONE YET? HERE, LET ME HELP YOU!

If you haven't bought your iPhone yet, or are exploring the options that you have available, this chapter is for you. During this chapter, we will discuss the features that differentiate iPhones, and help you decide what the best phone is for you.

In the last chapter, we learned about three main concepts; the fact that there are different types of phones, Face ID vs Touch ID, and the idea of operating systems.

There are a couple more iPhone-specific differentiating factors that you should think about when you are about to buy a new iPhone.

On the next page, I will put a true-to-life size comparison of what some of the popular phones and their size look like next to others. The size of your phone is probably the biggest factor you should consider when choosing a phone, because if the device that you buy is too small for you to use or see clearly, then you won't get very much out of using it, and it won't be as fun. For example, if you have poor eyesight, then getting a plus-sized phone might be beneficial to you.

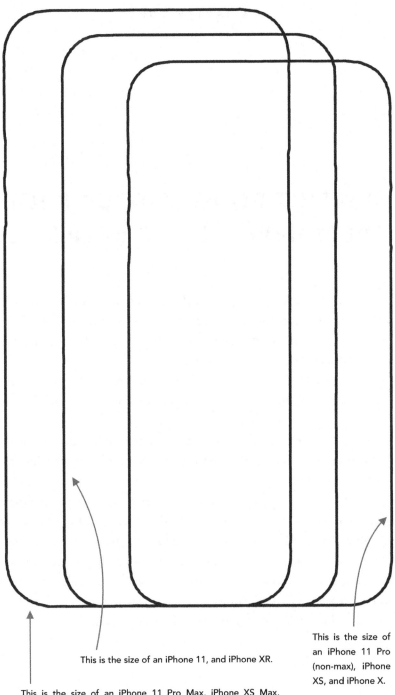

This is the size of an iPhone 11, and iPhone XR.

This is the size of an iPhone 11 Pro Max, iPhone XS Max, iPhone 8 Plus, iPhone 7 Plus, iPhone 6s Plus, and Phone 6 Plus.

This is the size of an iPhone 11 Pro (non-max), iPhone XS, and iPhone X.

This is the size of an iPhone SE (2016), iPhone 5, iPhone 5s, and iPhone 5c.

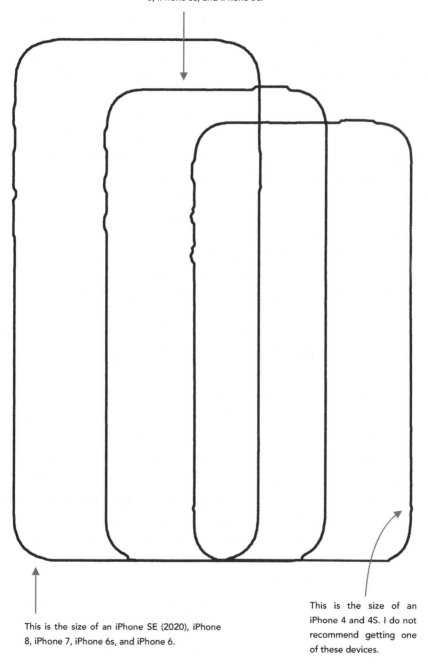

This is the size of an iPhone SE (2020), iPhone 8, iPhone 7, iPhone 6s, and iPhone 6.

This is the size of an iPhone 4 and 4S. I do not recommend getting one of these devices.

OUTDATED TECHNOLOGY

If you are choosing a phone you would like to buy, you might be intimidated by the sheer number of options that you have. However, about half of the options available you should probably avoid. This is because as technology gets older, the more outdated it becomes. If a piece of technology, like a phone for example, becomes outdated, it may become buggy, not work, or even unusable. Most of these older devices are hard to find anyway, and can't be purchased easily.

For that reason, I would avoid any of the phones that were released before the iPhone 6s (see the chart on page 6 for reference). All of the phones from the iPhone 6s to the most recent ones will work well enough for our purposes.

If you think that you will use your phone a lot, then I would try to get one of the newer devices.

For a light user (someone who doesn't use their phone that often), an iPhone 6s or iPhone 7 should be perfect for you.

There are a couple benefits to getting a newer device compared to the older ones:

1. Faster devices: When a new phone is released, it is typically faster than the phones that were released in the past. What this means, is that you can *do things* faster. You can open apps quicker, text quicker, etc. This might not seem like a big enough reason to purchase a newer device over an older one, but I promise you; a faster phone is so much better and makes the experience of using it so much more enjoyable.

2. Your device will last much longer: If you buy a newer device, it will last longer. You will get more *years* out of your device. Although newer devices cost more than older ones, they will last longer. Therefore, buying a newer device means that you will have to upgrade it much later down the road, compared to if you buy an older device (where you might have to upgrade it in a year or two).

3. Outdated software: If you buy an older phone, then it will (most likely) have an older version of software installed on it. "But wait! You told me I could just download a newer one and update it," you might be thinking, and I will explain why this isn't the case. When Apple

releases their newer updates, they "cut" one or two of the older phones from the group of devices that will be able to update to the newer software. Yes, it is a little disappointing, but Apple is saving those older devices; some of them just aren't capable of running the newer software.

4. Newer phones have generally better features: Each year, when Apple releases new phones, they improve them. Not only do they get faster, but they get some upgrades. The new iPhones might have better cameras, better speakers, better connectivity, etc. If you buy a newer phone, you might get some of these extra features that make the experience on the phone more enjoyable!

THE FINAL VERDICT: WHAT DO I RECOMMEND?

Well, this question is a little bit harder to answer than you'd think. It depends on what you're using it for, how much you will be using it, and other conditions that are specific to you.

For example, if you have poor eyesight, then I would recommend getting a plus-size phone. If you have small hands, then I would recommend getting a smaller phone.

Here is a list of some of the factors that you should think about before choosing what phone you want to purchase:

1. Size
2. Price-point
3. How new or how old the phone is
4. How much you think you will use the phone
5. The size of your hands or fingers
6. Getting the best 'bang for your buck'

After reading this chapter, I hope that you have a better understanding about the options that you have for a new phone, and how to decide what features/aspects are important to you!

CHAPTER FOUR

ACCESSORIZING YOUR PHONE; THE FUN PART

You just got your new phone, and you are so exciting to open the box and start learning more about it. But wait! Before you start using it, there are a couple of other things that you need to buy, in addition to the phone itself!

There are two accessories that you 100%, no questions asked, absolutely, need.

The first is a case for your phone. You have spent a lot of money on this device, and so you want to make sure that you protect it! For cases, you really can't go wrong; just about anything will do the job. If you want to be super protective, you can get a LifeProof case or an OtterBox case. These two brands typically offer the most protection. Apple also has cases available that they make for their phones. Personally, I use the Apple ones; they are slim, colorful, and feel super nice to the touch. I have also used LifeProof, OtterBox, Tech21, Spec, and other brands. Searching online, like on Amazon, is also another great place to buy a case.

The other accessory that you absolutely need is a screen protector for your phone. Screen protectors are like little transparent stickers that you can put on the front of your screen. There are many different types of screen protectors. I would recommend getting a glass one. Glass screen protectors act like a second piece of glass on the front of your display. If you drop it with the glass screen protector on and your screen shatters, your phone's real screen won't be shattered; just the glass screen protector. If this happens, you can just peel off the screen protector, buy another one, and apply it to your screen. You will be up and running in no time

If you are going to order accessories online, make sure that the accessory is for your specific device. Double, triple check! You don't want to order a case for an iPhone 5, if you have an iPhone XS Max. The phone sizes are different, and it won't fit.

Note: Some phones have the same size body/outer casing. For these models, the same case will fit on both devices. It will be clearly marked on the package, or in the title of the product if this is the case. If you make sure that your device is listed on the package or in the title of the product online, then you will be good to go.

There are other accessories for your phone that you might want to buy as well as accessories that you may have heard about. I will list them below, and give a little description of what the accessory is:

1. A portable charger: This is probably one of the most popular accessories that you can buy. A portable charger is a little device that will allow you to charge your phone when you do not have access to a wall outlet. Portable chargers are pretty neat and come in handy when your phone is about to die and you are away from an outlet!

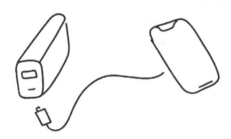

2. Another popular accessory, is a pop-socket. You don't have to buy one, but you might see them on someone else's phone. Pop-sockets are pieces of plastic that you can attach on the back of your phone. They can expand, which allows your fingers to slip through it and get a better grip on your phone. It is hard to explain using words, so I will include an image of one below:

3. Another cool accessory is a card-holder. These are rubber stickers that you can stick on the back of your phone. It is kind of like a mini-wallet, where you can slide cards (or cash) into the pocket. This way, your cards are always with you. A lot of my friends have them, and they will typically keep their license or debit card inside of them.

4. The last group of accessories are quite pricy. You probably won't buy them, but they are quite popular among younger people. The first, is an Apple device called an Apple Watch. An Apple Watch connects to your phone via bluetooth (bluetooth is just a way of connecting devices together and sending information between them without using wires). The Apple Watch acts like a regular watch, but also has a little digital screen on it where you can receive notifications on it, track workouts, and even call people! It is basically like a little computer on your wrist. Sometimes, they are called "smart watches". The other accessory that is quite popular among my friends and I, are AirPods. AirPods are similar to the headphones that were included in the box with your phone, but AirPods do not have wires, and essentially allow you to listen to music without the wires getting in your way. Similar to the Apple Watch, AirPods connect via bluetooth to your phone.

CHAPTER FIVE

iPHONE SETUP SEQUENCE

If you are unboxing your phone for the first time, you will have to go through the set-up process. The set-up process will ask questions like what language you want your phone to be in, as well as things like your WiFi information. This is fairly basic and easy to go through. Sometimes, the worker at the store will even go through the setup process with you so that you are ready to use your phone when you leave the store. If you have already set-up your iPhone, you can skip over the rest of this chapter if you'd like.

Another thing to note before we go through the set-up sequence, is that it has changed quite a bit over the different releases of iOS. Some of the steps might not be included in the book here, and maybe some of the steps I've included here in the book might not be in your set-up process. That is okay and normal, and you shouldn't worry about it. If a step in the process is unknown to you, read the words on the screen carefully, and make your best guess at what you should do to move forward.

STEP 1:

If you have just unboxed your iPhone, your phone's screen might be off. To turn it on, you can simply tap the power button on the right side of the phone. Once you do this, you will be prompted with a "Hello" screen. This is the beginning of the set-up process.

STEP 2:

The first question that it will ask you, is to choose your language. This will determine the language that all of the words on your phone will be. For this set up, I will choose English.

STEP 3:

The next thing that it will ask you, is to select your country.

STEP 4:

The next thing that it will ask you, is if you would like to use Quick Start. If you already have another iPhone that you have been using, you can quickly set it up by taking advantage of this feature (things like WiFi will be automatically inputted for you). If this is your first iPhone you can select "Set Up Manually".

STEP 5:

The next thing that it will have you set up, is WiFi.

Once you select the your WiFi router from the list shown above, it will prompt you to enter in the the router's password. If you do not know this, it can usually be found on the router box itself.

Once you enter in the password, you can hit the "Next" button in the top right corner. Once you do this, your phone will say that it will begin activating itself.

STEP 6:

The next step is regarding Data & Privacy. This is what the screen looks like:

You can just hit "Continue" here.

STEP 7:

The next thing that it will have you set up, is Touch ID or Face ID.

If you have a device with Touch ID, it will prompt you to repeatedly place your finger on the home button as it scans your fingerprint. This is 100% safe, and will make things like unlocking your phone easier. When you are setting this up, you don't have to push down on the button; you can just gently relax your finger on it. I would recommend using your thumb, but you could also use your index finger.

The finger that you are scanning with the fingerprint sensor is the finger that you will use to unlock your device. Therefore, use a finger that is comfortable to unlock your phone with.

While you are setting up Touch ID, you can read the instructions that are given on the top of the screen for help. If you are having trouble using Touch ID, you might not be holding your finger down on the scanner for long enough, or your hands might be wet. Both these things impair the scanner and make it harder to get a proper scan.

The phone that I am using for the demonstration in this book has Face ID, so we will be going through the setup of that in this example. This is what the screen looks like if you are going to set up Face ID:

After you click "Continue", it will prompt you to begin scanning your face. To do this, you will rotate your head in a circular motion. Begin with your head tilted upwards, then move your head to the left, then downwards, and finally to the right. You can see it register your face on the screen. Make sure that you are holding your phone parallel to your body for this to work properly. You should see your face on your screen (in a circle) if you your phone is scanning your face.

This is what it looks like to set up Face ID:

Once you scan your face once, you will have to do it a second time just to verify it.

The next step will ask you to set up a passcode for your phone:

Make sure that you can remember the passcode that you choose, because this is the passcode that will unlock your phone with. When unlocking your phone normally (once everything it set up), you will be prompted to use Touch ID or Face ID first. However, on rare occasions, you might have to enter in your phone's passcode. This is what you are setting up during this step. It is typically a 6-digit or 4-digit series of numbers. After you enter it in, it will ask you to enter it in again to verify it.

Tip: A helpful thing to do, is to start a little chart that will have all of your usernames and passwords to various accounts or other passwords that you may create while setting up your phone. Therefore, if you forget a password, you have a place to check!

STEP 9:

At this step, your phone will ask about Apps & Data, and how you would like to transfer apps and data to this iPhone. In other words, Apple is asking how you would like to import old data (from a previous iPhone if you've had one). If this is your first iPhone, then you can just tap "Don't Transfer Apps & Data". You may also just want to do this if you want to start fresh on your new phone.

I will choose "Don't Transfer Apps & Data".

At this next step, you will be instructed to enter in your Apple ID. An Apple ID is basically your "account" for your iPhone. This is what the screen looks like:

This is a major step, and probably one of the most important. An Apple ID is kind of like your account to the App Store. It is what allows you to buy apps, music, and other things.

If this is your first iPhone, or Apple device, chances are you will have to create one. If you need to create an Apple ID, click "Forgot password or don't have an Apple ID?". Then, you can click "Create a Free Apple ID".

Once you do this, you will be brought through a process of entering in information like your birthdate, name, etc.

Once you either create a new Apple ID, or enter in an old one, there will be a screen that says, "It may take a few minutes to set up your Apple ID"

STEP 11:

Now, there will be a screen that asks you to agree to Terms and Conditions. You can click "Agree" in the bottom right corner of your screen.

STEP 12:

The next couple of steps will ask you to answer the Express Settings questions. You can click the "Continue" button towards the bottom of your screen to begin answering the Express Settings questions.

STEP 13:

The first Express Setting, is about Updates on your phone. We will talk about updating your phone much later. You can just click the "Continue" button to proceed.

STEP 14:

The next step is regarding Apple Pay. I will talk more about this in a later chapter, but essentially Apple Pay is a way of having your credit/debit card always on your phone and available to use at stores for purchases.

Another reason why it might be beneficial to set up your credit or debit card on your phone, is so you can buy apps that cost money on the App Store, or things like Movies and TV shows.

If you set up your credit card now, it will make setting up other things later much easier!

STEP 15:

This step is about Siri. We will talk about Siri later in this book. You can simply press "Continue" here to proceed.

After you press continue, it might ask if you want to "Improve Siri & Dictation". Personally, I would choose "Not now", which can be found at the bottom of your screen. If you press "Share Audio Recordings", then you would be allowing Apple to store audio of your Siri and Dictations. Again, personally I would choose "Not now".

STEP 16:

This next step is regarding Screen Time. This feature isn't really important (because we won't really be monitoring how long we use our phone), so we can just click, "Continue".

STEP 17:

We are almost done, I promise!

This screen will ask if you want to share your App Analytics with Apple. Again, you can choose if you want to share it with Apple, but I would personally just choose "Don't Share".

STEP 18:

This next step will teach you a little bit about what True Tone Display is. You can just click "Continue" at the bottom of your screen to proceed through the set up process.

Here is one option that you might not have, depending on what version of iOS software your phone has.

This screen is giving you the option if you want your phone to be in Light Mode, or Dark Mode.

There isn't much of a difference, and there isn't any real reason why you would want to choose one over the other (besides aesthetic purposes). If you want your phone's interface to be generally be light and bright, then you can choose Light Mode. If you want your phone's interface to be generally dark and black, then you can choose Dark Mode.

If you are curious, I use Light Mode, and will be using it for the demonstrations in the rest of this book.

One of the last things that it will ask, is to choose which "Display Zoom" mode you want. You can choose between "Standard", and "Zoomed". You can also look at various example images, where it will show you both options side by side. The only main difference between the two options, is that the "Zoomed" option makes things, like App Icons, larger. If you have poor eyesight, you can choose the zoomed option, and it will make things a little bit easier to see.

Note: Choosing the "Zoomed" view doesn't have an affect on the size of the text on your phone. We will talk about how to increase (or decrease) the size of your phone's text in a later chapter. Choosing the zoomed option mostly changes things like App Icons and other things that are displayed on the screen.

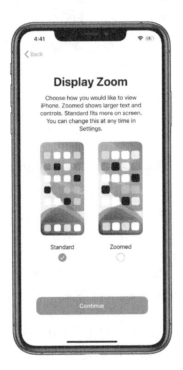

STEP 21:

The last three screens of the set-up process will teach you three of the general/basic functions. We will go into more depth with these functions (and a lot more) in another chapter though!

Once the set-up process is complete, you will be shown the homepage of your new phone.

WRAPPING UP THE CHAPTER...

Congratulations! Your phone is all set up! This is super exciting! I'm so excited to teach you more about everything you can do!

But before we learn some of the gestures and functions, let's talk about the other things that you can find in the box that your phone came in!

CHAPTER SIX

YOUR PHONE BOX

Inside of the box that your phone came in, you will see various things. You should have a little packet of literature (this has the phone's manual and pieces of written information), a charging cord, wired headphones, a wall power adapter (the little white cube), and a short dongle.

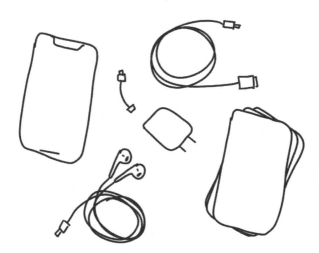

The charger and wall adapter cube are used to charge your phone. The battery on your phone will probably last a full day, maybe even two. I would recommend charging your phone every night when you go to bed. This will ensure that your phone's battery is full every morning when you wake up, and will last you through the day up until you go to bed. The battery indicator is found on the top right hand side of the device. Of the two pictures below, the picture on the left is the indicator showing that the battery is full, or at 100% capacity. The picture on the right is the indicator that the battery is charging. This indicator will change based on your battery percentage, and will slowly decrease throughout the day as your phone's battery decreases. (We will talk more about indicators later in the book.)

There is also a set of wired headphones (called EarPods) that are included in the box. You can plug these into the port on the bottom of your phone. If your phone has a 3.5mm headphone jack (the 3.5mm headphone jack is a small round hole that is in the bottom left or top of the phone; it was removed in the iPhone 7 and all of the newer models since), the you plug your 3.5mm pair of headphones into the 3.5mm headphone jack. If you have a newer device, however, you do not have a 3.5mm headphone jack. Therefore, your headphones have a lightning plug on the end, and plug directly into the lightning port in the bottom of the phone. Headphones can be used to listen to music, watch movies, or watch videos on your phone.

The dongle that may or may not be included in your box is an adapter. This dongle is about three inches, and converts an Apple lightning port to 3.5mm headphone jack port. On one end, it has a lighting-port male plug. This is used to plug into the bottom of your device. On the other end, you have a 3.5mm female port. This allows you to plug in a pair of 3.5mm headphones, or an aux cord, into your phone.

If you do not have a different pair of headphones that use a 3.5mm headphone jack or an aux cord, then you do not have to worry about this dongle.

Lastly, your phone box will include a small packet of literature. If you slide the pieces of paper out, you will see a couple of different things, like general information for your device, a user guide, some Apple

Stickers, and maybe a sim-card ejector (the metal piece that kind of looks like a bent paper-clip).

WHAT IS A LIGHTNING PORT?

The lightning port is the port on the bottom of your device. It is centered in the middle, and has a rectangular/ovular shape. This lightning port is mainly used for charing your device. However, if you do not have a 3.5mm headphone jack on your device, then you use this same lightning port to plug in your headphones (or the dongle) to listen to music or watch movies/videos.

That is everything that is included in the box, and their main functions. As you read through this book, you might start to realize that a lot of things overlap, and there are a lot of different ways to do the same thing on your phone. It is normal to feel a little lost and overwhelmed when you are first getting started. But with a little bit of patience and some practice, I know that you will get used to it! In the next chapter, we will talk about your device, the physical buttons on it, and some of the other outside features of your phone.

CHAPTER SEVEN

EXPLORING THE OUTSIDE FEATURES OF YOUR PHONE

Your new iPhone is probably unlike anything you've ever used before. It is different than electronics like your TV or computer. Your phone has three or four buttons (depending on if you have a home button or not). That also means that most of the interactions will be carried out by using the screen, coupled with a few simple gestures.

USING GESTURE CONTROLS

There are four basic gestures that you should learn so that you can interact with your phone properly:

1. Tapping your screen: When you click on things, like app icons for example, you are going to be tapping the screen of your phone. You don't have to push hard for phone to register your finger; you can just lightly tap it.

2. Swiping: To swipe on your phone, you will glide your finger across your display from one place to another. The direction of your swipe will determine where the contents of the screen go. For example, if you swipe upwards on your screen when browsing a webpage, the webpage will move underneath your finger and allow you to move the webpage's content upwards. This is similar to how you scroll on a

computer.

3. Touching and holding: There are two (main) places where this gesture is used. The first is in control center. We will learn more about control center in the next chapter, and how we use this gesture there. The other place where we will use touching and holding, is on the home screen (the place where all of your app icons are found). We will learn more about touching and holding on the home screen when we talk about customizing your home screen!

4. Pinching to zoom: If you want to zoom in on a photo to see more detail, for example, you can place two fingers on your screen, and move your fingers farther apart from each other. You can also move your fingers closer together to zoom back out. (Pinch your fingers together = zoom out; move your fingers apart = zoom in)

USING THE ON-SCREEN KEYBOARD

While we are on the subject of gesture controls for your phone, lets briefly talk about the on-screen keyboard that you will use to input text onto your phone. This is what it looks like:

Typically, there are two main ways to type on your screen, and it usually depends on the way that you hold your phone. Typically, people hold their phone in one of two ways:

Using one hand to hold the device, and using a pointer finger to navigate the interface.

Using two hands to hold the device and using both thumbs to navigate the interface.

Now, of course you can hold your phone in any way that you want and use whatever method is comfortable for you to navigate the interface.

If you are holding your phone with one hand, and using your index finger to navigate your phone, then you would use your index finger to type on the screen. However, if you hold your phone with both hands, then you would type with both of your thumbs. Again, you can hold your phone and type on it how ever you would like, but these are the two most popular ways. Personally, I hold my phone with two hands and type with both my thumbs. Using this method is a little bit harder, but you can type much faster with it.

THE REAL, PHYSICAL BUTTONS ON YOUR PHONE

Now that you know how to interact with your screen, we can talk about the buttons on the outside of your phone. On the next page I will attach a photo of a phone and I will identify the various buttons and ports around the device.

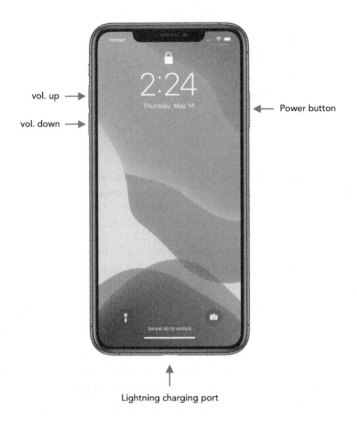

vol. up

vol. down

Power button

Lightning charging port

This phone does not have a home button.

If you have a home button, here is where it is located (not all iPhones have home buttons):

If you have an iPhone SE (2016) or older, then you have a 3.5mm headphone jack (the headphone jack is also found on the iPhone SE 2020 version). This can be found on the bottom left corner of your phone (like the picture above), or on the top right corner of the phone (depending on what phone you have).

CHARGING

Lastly, to charge your phone, you will use the charger that came in your phone's box. You can plug the smaller lightning end into the bottom of your phone, and plug the slightly bigger USB end into the wall-adapter cube. This wall-adapter cube can be plugged directly into the wall. Now, your phone should be charging!

GENERAL FUNCTIONS AND OPERATIONS - PHONES WITH TOUCH ID

To make things easier, I have divided this topic into two sections.
Chapter 8: Functions for a phone with Touch ID
Chapter 9: Functions for a phone with Face ID

I think that dividing this topic up into these two sections will make the information that you need to know more available and easier to understand. If you are still confused about which of the two categories your device falls into, you can look at the images in chapter two. If your device has a circular button on the bottom of the screen, then you have Touch ID. If your phone has the notch on the top of the display and doesn't have a home button, then you have Face ID.

Therefore, if you have a phone that uses Face ID, please skip to chapter nine. If you have a phone with Touch ID, read this chapter, but feel free to skip chapter nine and move straight to chapter ten (don't worry; the content is the same. Splitting this into two different chapters just makes the information more tailored to your specific device).

Before you use some of the apps and features on your phone, you have to know basic functions and gestures. We will go through these slowly and in different sections. Try to practice these gestures and basic functions, because you will be using them daily to navigate the phone's interface!

LOCKING AND UNLOCKING YOUR PHONE

The first basic function, is unlocking your phone. To lock or unlock your phone, you will press the power button on the right side of the device (if you have an older device, like an iPhone 5, it might be on the top of the device). Pressing the power button once will wake your screen up. If you press it again, it will turn the screen off.

Once you wake the device up, you should see a screen that says the time at the top, and the date underneath it. This is the lock screen (a picture of my lock screen is shown on the next page). This is also a handy way to see the time on your phone. This screen will also show notifications when they come in. Notifications are alerts that your phone is letting you know about. For example, you might have a notification that says you have received a text message. You might also have a notification that says you have missed a call. Maybe you have received a notification about a news headline. These notifications will be shown on the lock screen.

Here is a picture of a lock screen. As you can see, the time is 4:38, and I have one notification, a text message, from my dad.

Note: If you have an iPhone with a home button, you can also use the home button to wake the device up (but you cannot use it to lock the phone - you would have to use the power button to do that).

All of these iPhones also have a fancy feature where every time you raise the phone, it will automatically wake up and show you your lock screen.

We have learned how to wake the device up, but to unlock your device, you will have to use either Touch ID or your password that you set up during the set-up process. To begin, wake your device up. Place your finger on the fingerprint scanner (on the home button), and your iPhone will unlock.

Sometimes, if your finger is sweaty, wet, or not aligned correctly, your phone might vibrate and have you try again. If your fingerprint keeps being mis-read, the phone will just prompt you to enter your passcode (the 6 or 4 digit one that we set up during the set-up process).

This is normal, and isn't something to worry about.

Now that your phone is unlocked, you are in!

To lock your phone, you have to press the power button on the right side of the device (if you have an older device, like an iPhone 5, it might be on the top). This is the only way to lock your phone.

> Note: After a minute or two of your phone being idle (not used), your phone will lock itself automatically. This is called auto-lock, and it is normal. Your phone isn't dead; your phone has just temporarily locked itself (if your phone's screen was on all the time, your battery on the device would drain very quickly; this feature is just to preserve battery life!).

RETURNING TO YOUR HOME SCREEN

The "home screen", is the default view of your phone; it is where you can see all of your app icons. If you have just set up your phone, or haven't downloaded any apps yet, you will only see the default apps that Apple downloads onto your phone for you. I will go into more detail about downloading apps and customizing the app layout on your home screen later. If you are inside of and app and want to return home, you will push the circular home button on the bottom of your screen.

Returning "home" from an app is probably one of the most used gestures on my phone.

CHANGING YOUR VOLUME

On the left side of your device, you will find two buttons that are stacked, one on top of the other. These are the volume buttons. The button on the top is the "volume up" button, and the button below it is "volume down" button. These can be used to turn the volume up or down. When you press either of these two buttons, you will see an indicator show up somewhere on the screen that your volume has changed.

The two volume buttons are shown here. The top one is volume up, ad the bottom one is volume down.

vol. up ⟶

vol. down ⟶

MULTITASKING VIEW & QUITTING APPS

When you open an app, it stays open in the "background". This is so you can multitask and go back to it without having to wait for it to re-load. It is a pretty neat concept. To enter the multitasking view (also known as the app switcher), you simply double click the home button. This will bring up this screen:

If you want to multitask, you can swipe between the different "cards". If you want to switch back to an app that was previously open, you can just tap on that app's 'card'. However, this is rather complicated, and I don't really use this multitasking feature.

However, one thing that you might want to do, is quit the apps that you have open. This is kind of important. To quit apps, you first have to get to the multitasking view by double clicking the home button. Next, you can just swipe upwards on each "card". They should go flying upwards. This will quit the app. This is different from simply closing the app, where you would just click the home button (to return to the home screen). Once every app is quit, you will be returned to the home screen automatically.

CONTROL CENTER

Control center is an important feature. Here, you have quick access to toggles, or buttons, where you can do quick tasks. Things like changing your brightness, turning on airplane mode, auto-orientation locking your screen, and turning on do-not disturb mode can all be found here. Don't worry; I will talk about what each of those things mean in a little bit. First, you need to know how to access control center. To do this, simply swipe up from the bottom of your screen.

Now, you might be like, "Wait a minute! Mine looks different!" And that is okay. The cool thing is that you are able to completely customize the layout of the controls that are found in the control center! This is how I've customized my layout, but you can customize it however you'd like. But we will worry about that much, much, much, later! For now, let's just get the basics down.

Here, you can see a variety of controls to pick from. It almost looks like those large control panels used in spaceships in movies and stuff! Each one of these controls do different things and we will walk through them together.

This box, found in the top left of the corner of the control center, houses various toggles that have to do with connectivity. The top left icon is for toggling on and off airplane mode. When Airplane Mode is turned on, you cannot receive calls or other notifications on your phone; it basically turns off your cellular connection and WiFi. The top right icon is for turning your cellular data on or off. The bottom left icon is for turning WiFi on or off. The bottom right icon is for turning bluetooth on or of.

This box is used for music controls. Here you can play/pause, go back a song, or skip to the next song.

This toggle is for turning Orientation Lock on or off. If you click it, the orientation of your phone will be locked. For example, if you are using your phone portrait (holding it normally, with the home button at the bottom), and you turn Orientation Lock on, your phone's screen will stay in the portrait orientation even if you rotate your phone around.

This toggle is for Do Not Disturb. This means that calls, messages, notifications, or other alerts will not show up in your notifications (you will still receive them, they just won't show up on your lockscreen or make noise). This is handy if you need to be distraction-free!

This is the flashlight toggle. If you click it, you will turn the flashlight on. You can click it again to turn it back off.

This is the timer button. If you click on this, it will open the Clock App, and it will automatically jump to the timer tab of this app. This is a quick and easy way to access the timer.

This is the calculator button. Similar to the timer button, it will jump straight to the Calculator app when you click it.

This is the Camera app shortcut. When you click it, you will jump straight to the Camera app. Personally, I just click the Camera app icon that is found on my home page.

This is the brightness toggle. You can interact with it by sliding your finger up and down along the toggle. This will increase (gradually swiping up along the toggle) or decrease (gradually swiping down along the toggle) your phone's brightness as you move your finger across it. This is the fastest way to change your phone's brightness.

Note: Something to note about the brightness of your phone, is that your phone might have a setting called auto brightness turned on. This means that your screen's brightness will automatically adjust based on the environment that you are in. Sometimes this is good, but sometimes it is bad. Personally, I have this turned off. We will learn about how to do this in a future chapter.

The last toggle that we will discuss, is the volume toggle. Similar to how the brightness toggle works, the volume will increase (gradually swiping up along the toggle) or decrease (gradually swiping down along the toggle) your volume as you move your finger across this toggle. Do you remember what the other way to increase or decrease the volume on your phone is? Thats right; use the physical buttons on the left side of your device!

The other toggles that I have in my control center on my phone are specific to me and things that I use. Again, we will learn about how to customize this later and how to add more controls to it if you'd like to.

There is something else about control center that makes it even more powerful. If you press and hold on any of these toggles, it will enlarge the toggle, or give more options, like additional buttons, that you can interact with. I will put some examples of what this looks like below:

In this example, I pressed and held on the volume toggle. This enlarged it, and allows me to fine-tune the volume of my device.

In this example, I pressed and held on the music toggle. This enlarged it, and brought up the option to jump to a specific place in the song, as well as volume control.

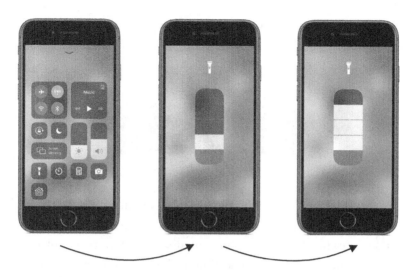

In this example, I pressed and held on the flashlight toggle. This enlarged it, and allowed me to fine-tune the brightness of the flashlight by sliding up and down the increments on the enlarged toggle.

Wow! That was a pretty dense section of this chapter. Hopefully you are still with me after all that! You did amazing! At first, this might seem a little crazy and seem like a lot of information, but most of the toggle's icons look like their function, so it will be easy to remember them. If you can't remember them at first, thats ok! After spending time with the toggles and playing around with them, they will become second nature to you!

You may not even use control center, and that is also okay. I'm gonna be honest with you again: I might only use the control center a dozen times a day. The controls that are most important and the ones that you will probably use the most, are airplane mode, brightness, volume, and the flashlight.

THE STATUS BAR

Towards the top of your phone, you will see a couple of small indicators. These indicators make up the status bar. The status bar is shown pretty much all the time at the top of your phone. The layout of these status icons will change based on the type of phone that you have, but the symbols all mean the same thing. This is what the status bar on my phone looks like:

This first symbol (in the top left) looks like steps. Basically, this icon lets you know if you are able to make and receive calls. It also shows how close you are to cell towers (and if you are able to make a connection to them). However, if you do not have signal, it will simply read "No Signal".

The next icon is my service provider. For me, it says "AT&T".

The next icon is the WiFi icon. If you see this icon, it means that you are connected to WiFi. Depending on what phone you have, you might also see the word "Wi-Fi".

The next icon, is the little loading sign. If you see this icon, it means that there is network activity going on. For example, if you are browsing the web, then you might see this icon shown in the status bar, because you are accessing the internet.

The next icon, centered in the middle, is the time.

This icon means that there is an app or website that is using my location.

The last icon shown, is my battery percentage. This shows the status of my battery both visually and numerically, and lets me known if I need to charge my phone or not.

If you are not connected to WiFi, you might have a LTE, 5G, 4G, 3G, GPRS, or E symbol shown. These symbols represent varying degrees of connectivity to the internet (this is what determines if you are able to look something up or not). These indicators can be found here:

Now, we will talk about some of the other icons that might show up on your status bar, but aren't specifically shown on mine.

The first icon is airplane mode. If you see this icon, it means that you can't make/receive calls, send/receive texts, or use the internet because airplane mode is turned on.

If you see this little alarm clock icon, it means that you have an alarm set. Unfortunately for me, my alarm is usually set for 6:30 am.

This is the orientation lock icon. If you see this icon, it means that orientation lock is turned on (reference back to page 60 to learn more about orientation lock).

This icon is for Do Not Disturb. This means that calls, messages, notifications, or other alerts will not show up in your notifications.

If you see this icon, it means that you have headphones plugged into your phone.

These are the most important status icons that you should know about.

There is one last aspect to the status bar that we will discuss. When you are doing different tasks, the status bar may change colors. If you are calling somebody for example, the status bar will turn green. If you are using a personal hotspot, or your phone is accessing your location, it will turn blue. If you are recording audio, it will turn red.

THE RING SWITCH

The ring switch is a small switch that can be found just above the volume buttons. Flipping it back and forth switches between ring mode (where alerts will make noise when they come in), and silent mode (where your phone will just vibrate when alerts come in, and won't make any noise). Being a student, my phone is on silent mode while I'm at school, so that it doesn't make any noise and disrupt class. However, when I am back at home, I may want alerts to "ding" when they come in, and so I can always just flip the ring switch to change to ring mode.

If you look closely at the ring switch, you can see that when you are switched into silent mode, the inside of the switch is colored orange. This is another way of knowing which mode you are in.

Ring switch →

No Service   20%

4:27
Thursday, May 14

POWERING YOUR PHONE OFF AND BACK ON

When you lock your phone, you aren't powering it down. You are merely putting it to sleep. Locking your phone is almost like shutting your eyes; you aren't quite asleep yet, but you're resting, saving energy.

To power down your device, and to shut it completely, 100% off, you have to press and hold the power button.

Once you hold this button down for long enough, you will be prompted to either "slide to power off" or "cancel". If you want to power your device down, then you can slide the "slide to power off" toggle (at the top of your screen) to the right, and your phone will begin to power itself down. If you didn't mean to hold down the power button, you can simple click the "cancel" button at the bottom of the screen.

When you shut off your phone, you won't receive texts, calls, alerts, or any other notifications. It is almost like your phone is "temporarily dead".

To power your phone back on, you can simply hold the power button down until the glowing apple logo shows up on your screen.

If you press and hold the power button to power on your phone, but your phone's battery is completely dead, you will be shown an icon with a battery that is empty. At this point, you will have to plug your phone into a charger if you want to continue using your phone.

THE EMERGENCY SOS FEATURE

iPhones have a way to easily call emergency services if you need to. To activate Emergency SOS, press the power button five times. You will then be prompted to either "slide to power off" or "cancel" (just like powering down), but because you clicked the power button five times, you will have an additional option for "Emergency SOS". You can swipe right on this, and it will begin to call the emergency service for your correct location (depending got where you live).

Congratulations! You made it through this chapter! The gestures that you have learned in this chapter are the fundamentals of working your new iPhone. I hope that it was fun to play with them, and that you weren't frustrated!

If you want more practice using the gestures explained in this chapter, feel free to jump back to sections, re-read them, and practice some more! Practice makes perfect, and practice is key to becoming fluent with your new phone!

In the rest of this book, we will learn about specific apps, their purposes, and how to do different things in them. I will mainly stick to the apps that are automatically downloaded on all iPhones (the ones that are made by Apple).

You're doing great so far! You've come a long way from where you were when you first picked up your phone. I can guarantee that you will continue learning more and having fun!

Because I split this topic into two different sections, you can skip the next chapter, and move on to chapter ten! (This next chapter has the same content that you just read, but geared towards phones with Face ID).

GENERAL FUNCTIONS AND OPERATIONS - PHONES WITH FACE ID

This chapter has the exact same information as the previous chapter, just geared towards phones with Face ID.

Before you use some of the apps and features on your phone, you have to know basic functions and gestures. We will go through these slowly and in different sections. Try to practice these gestures and basic functions, because you will be using them daily to navigate the phone's interface!

LOCKING AND UNLOCKING YOUR PHONE

The first basic function, is unlocking your phone. To lock or unlock your phone, you will press the power button on the right side of the device. Pressing the power button once will wake your screen up. If you press it again, it will turn the screen off.

Once you wake the device up, you should see a screen that says the time at the top, and the date underneath it (or the percentage that your phone is charged). This is the lock screen (a picture of my lock screen is shown on the next page). This is also a handy way to see the time on your phone. This screen will also show notifications when they come in. Notifications are alerts that your phone is letting you know about. For example, you might have a notification that says you have received a text message. You might also have a notification that says you have missed a call. Maybe you have received a notification about a news headline. These notifications will be shown on the lock screen.

Here is a picture of my lock screen. As you can see, the time is 9:47, and I have one notification, a text message, from my dad.

Note: If you have an iPhone with Face ID (one with a notch on the top), you can simply double-tap the screen to wake it up (but you cannot double tap to lock the phone - you would have to use the power button to do that).

All of these iPhones also have a fancy feature where every time you raise the phone, it will automatically wake up and show you your lock screen.

We have learned how to wake the device up, but to unlock your device, you will have to use either Face ID or your password that you set up during the set-up process. To begin, wake your device up. Next, simply look at your phone and swipe upwards from the bottom bar (you can see what the bottom rectangular bar looks like in the image on the previous page).

Now that your phone is unlocked, you are in!

To lock your phone, the only way to do it is to press the power button on the right side of the device.

> Note: After a minute or two of your phone being idle (not used), your phone will lock itself automatically. This is called auto-lock, and it is normal. Your phone isn't dead; your phone has just temporarily locked itself (If your phone's screen was on all the time, your battery on the device would drain very quickly; this feature is to preserve battery life!).

TROUBLE SHOOTING FOR FACE ID

Over time, I have noticed that Face ID can be a little finicky at times.

The first thing that I noticed that can help Face ID recognize your face, is to pick up your phone and hold it semi-parallel to my body when you try to unlock it. For example, if my phone is on the table, and I wake it up (either by clicking the power button or double tapping the screen), the Face ID might not register my face. This is shown in the first image on the next page. However, if I hold it semi-parallel to my face, my face will be registered through Face ID. This is shown in the second image:

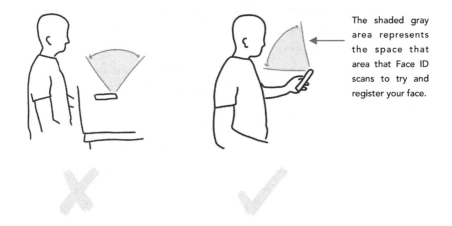

The shaded gray area represents the space that area that Face ID scans to try and register your face.

Another thing I noticed, is that if I am bundled up (too much of my face is covered), then Face ID might not recognize.

However, something that is interesting, is that Face ID will adapt to when the appearance of your face changes over time. For example, let's say you get a hair cut. Your Face ID will still work. Just bought a new pair of glasses? Face ID will still work. It is pretty cool!

If you keep trying everything, and your face is just still not being registered, then after a second or two, your phone will just prompt you to enter in your password to unlock your phone.

RETURNING TO YOUR HOME SCREEN

The "home screen", is the default view of your phone; it is where you can see all of your app icons. If you have just set up your phone, or haven't downloaded any apps yet, you will only find the default apps that Apple downloads onto your phone for you. I will go into more detail about downloading apps and customizing your app layout on your home screen later. If you are inside of and app and want to return home, simply swipe up from the bottom of your device by swiping upwards on the little bar at the bottom. This bar is known as the home indicator bar.

Returning "home" from an app is probably one of the most used gestures on my phone.

CHANGING YOUR VOLUME

On the left side of your device, you will find two buttons that are stacked, one on top of the other. These are the volume buttons. The one on top is the "volume up" button, and the button below it is "volume down" button. These can be used to turn the volume up or down. When you press either of these two buttons, you will see an indicator show up somewhere on the screen that your volume has changed.

The two volume buttons are shown stacked here. The top one is volume up, ad the bottom one is volume down.

vol. up →

vol. down →

MULTITASKING VIEW & QUITTING APPS

When you open an app, it stays open in the "background". This is so you can multitask and go back to it without having to wait for it to re-load. It is a pretty neat concept. To enter the multitasking view (also known as the app switcher), you swipe upwards on the home indicator bar (at the bottom of the screen) and hold for about a second (keep your finger on the screen). You will feel a little vibrate, and soon the multitasking screen will be shown. If you have any apps open, their "cards" will pop up. Once these cards come up, you can pick up your finger off of the screen. You should see this on your screen:

If you want to multitask, you can swipe between the different "cards". If you want to switch back to an app that you once had open, you can just tap on that app's 'card'. However, this is rather complicated, and I don't really use multitasking.

However, one thing that you might want to do, is quit the apps that you have open. This is kind of important. To quit apps, you first have to get to the multitasking view. Swipe up from the bottom, and hold for a second. Once it vibrates and the "cards" pop up, you can release your finger. Now, you can just swipe upwards on each "card". It should go flying upwards. This will quit the app. This is different from simply closing the app, where you would just click the swipe upwards on the home indicator bar rather quickly. For multitasking and quitting apps, you hold your finger down on the screen for a second (after swiping up) before releasing your finger. Once every app is quit, you will be returned to the home screen automatically.

CONTROL CENTER

Control center is an important feature. Here, you have quick access to toggles, or buttons, that can do quick tasks. Things like changing your brightness, turning on airplane mode, auto-orientation locking your screen, and turning on do-not disturb mode can all be found here. Don't worry; I will talk about what those things mean in a little bit. First, you need to know how to access control center. To do this, reach all the way to the top right corner of your display (the little area between the notch and the right side of the screen), and then pull downwards a little.

Now, you might be like wait a minute! Mine looks different! And that is okay. The cool thing is that you are able to completely customize it! This is how I've customized my layout, but you can customize it however you'd like. But we will worry about that much, much, much, later! For now, let's just get the basics down.

Here, you can see a variety of controls to pick from. It almost looks like those large control panels used in spaceships in movies and stuff! Each one of these controls do different things, and we will walk through them together.

This box in the top left of the control center houses various toggles that have to do with connectivity. The top left icon is for toggling on and off airplane mode. Airplane mode makes it so the you cannot receive calls or other notifications to your phone; it basically turns off your cellular connection and WiFi. The top right icon is for turning on and off your cellular data. This is a quick and easy way to turn it off if your limit is reached! The bottom left icon is for toggling on and off WiFi. The bottom right icon is for toggling on and off bluetooth.

This box is for music controls. Here you can play/pause, go back a song, or skip to the next song.

This toggle is for turning on/off orientation lock. If you click this, it will lock the way that your phone is oriented. For example, if you are using your phone portrait (up and down), and you turn it on, then your phone's screen will stay in this orientation even if you turn the phone on its side.

This toggle is for do not disturb. This means that calls, messages, notifications, or other alerts will not show up in your notifications. This is handy if you need to be in a place where you need to be distraction-free!

This is the flashlight toggle. If you click it, it will turn the flashlight on and off.

This is the timer button. If you click on this, it will open the Clock App, and it will automatically jump to the timer tab of this app. It is a neat and quick way to access the timer.

This is the calculator button. Similar to the timer button, if you click this calculator button, it will jump straight to the calculator app. This is the fastest way to access the calculator.

This is the camera shortcut app. This will jump straight to the camera app. Personally, I just click the camera app that is on my home page.

This is the brightness toggle. You can interact with this toggle, and slide up and down along the toggle. This will increase (gradually swiping up along the toggle) or decrease (gradually swiping down along the toggle) your phone's brightness as you move your finger across this toggle. This is the fastest way to change your brightness.

Note: Something to note about the brightness of your phone, is that your phone might have auto brightness turned on. This means that your screen's brightness will automatically adjust depending on the environment that you you are in. Sometimes this is good, but sometimes it is bad. Personally, I have this turned off. We will learn about how to do this in a future chapter.

The last toggle that we will discuss, is the volume toggle. Similar to how the brightness toggle works, the volume will increase (gradually swiping up along the toggle) or decrease (gradually swiping down along the toggle) your volume as you move your finger across this toggle. Do you remember what the other way to increase or decrease the volume on your phone is? Thats right; use the physical buttons on the left side of your device!

The other toggles that I have activated on my phone are specific to me, and things that I use. Again, we will learn about how to customize this later and how to add more controls to it if you'd like to.

There is something else about control center that makes it even more powerful. If you press and hold on any of these toggles, it will enlarge the toggle, or give more options, like additional buttons, that you can interact with. I will put some examples below:

 →

In this example, I pressed and held on the volume toggle. This enlarged it, and allows me to fine-tune the volume.

In this example, I pressed and held on the music toggle. This enlarged it, and brought up the option to jump to a specific place in the song, as well as volume control.

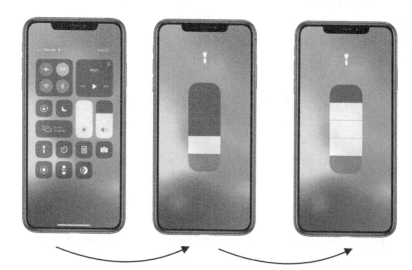

In this example, I pressed and held on the flashlight toggle. This enlarged it, and allowed me to fine-tune the brightness of the flashlight by sliding up and down the increments on the enlarged toggle.

Wow! That was a pretty dense section of this chapter. Hopefully you are still with me after all that! You did amazing! At first, this might seem a little crazy and seem like a lot of information, but most of the toggle's icons look like their function, so it will be easy to remember. If you can't remember them, thats ok! Im gonna let you in on a little secret: sometimes I don't even remember what they do. But you will learn them, and they will become second nature, just like most of them have become to me!

You may not even use control center, and that is also okay. Im gonna be honest with you again; I might only use control center a dozen times a day. The controls that are most important, and the ones that you will probably use the most, are airplane mode, brightness, volume, and the flashlight.

THE STATUS BAR

On the top of your phone, you can see small indicators. These indicators make up the status bar. The status bar is shown pretty much all the time on your phone, at the top. The layout of these status icons will change based on the type of phone that you have, but the symbols all mean the same thing. This is what my status bar looks like:

The first icon (in the top left) is the time.

The next symbol looks like steps. This icon means that you are able to make and receive calls, and shows how close you are to cell towers (and if you are able to make a connection to them). However, if you do not have signal, it will simply read "No Signal".

The next icon, is the Wifi icon. This just means that you are connected to WiFi.

The last icon shown, is my battery percentage. This shows visually and numerically the status of my battery, and if I need to charge my phone or not. At this specific point, my phone's battery was low, and it was charging.

If you are not connected to WiFi, you might have an LTE, 5G, 4G, 3G, GPRS, or E symbol. These symbols represent varying degrees of connectivity to the internet. This is what determines if you can look something up or not. These other indicators could look something like this:

Now, we will talk about some of the other icons that might show up on your status bar, but isn't shown specifically on mine.

The first is airplane mode. This means that you can't make/receive calls, send/receive texts, or use the internet until you turn it back off. You can use this while traveling on a plane, or as an easy way to conserve battery life!

This little alarm clock means that I have an alarm set. Unfortunately for me, my alarm is usually set for 6:30am.

This is the orientation lock icon. This means that your screen will not rotate around if you turn it.

This icon is for Do Not Disturb. This means that calls, messages, notifications, or other alerts will not show up in your notifications. This is handy if you need to be in a place where you need to be distraction-free!

If you see this icon, it means that you have headphones plugged in.

The next icon, is the little loading sign. This means that there is a webpage that is loading or other network activity is going on in the background.

This icon means that there is an app or website that is using my location.

These are the main and most important status icons that you should know.

There is one last aspect to the status bar. Do you remember how the time is shown in the top left corner? Well, sometimes there might be a rectangular/ovular shape that surrounds the time when you are doing specific tasks.

It will look like this:

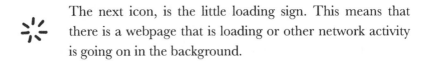

The shape around the time will change color based on the task the you are doing. If you are calling somebody, it will be green. If you are using a personal hotspot, or accessing your location, it will turn blue. If you are recording audio, it will turn red.

THE RING SWITCH

The ring switch is a small switch just above the volume buttons. Flipping it back and forth switches between ring mode (where alerts will make noise when they come in), and silent mode (where your phone will just vibrate, and won't make no noise). Being a student, my phone is on silent mode while I'm at school, so that it doesn't make any noise and disrupt class. However, when I am back at home, I may want alerts to "ding" when they come in, and so I can always just flip the ring switch to change to ring mode.

If you look closely at the ring switch, you can see that when you are switched into silent mode, the inside of the switch is colored orange. This is another way of knowing which mode you are in.

Ring switch →

POWERING YOUR PHONE OFF AND BACK ON

When you lock your phone, you aren't powering it down. You are merely putting it to sleep. Locking your phone is almost like shutting your eyes; you aren't quite asleep yet, but you're resting, saving energy.

To power down your device, and to shut it completely, 100% off, you have to press and hold the power button, as well as one of the volume buttons.

Volume button →

← Power button

Once you hold these two buttons down for long enough, you will be prompted to either "slide to power off", "Emergency SOS", or "cancel". If you want to power your device down, then you can slide the "slide to power off" toggle at the top of your screen, to the right, and your phone will begin to power itself down. We will talk about the

Emergency SOS feature in the next section. If you didn't mean to hold down the buttons, you can simple click the "cancel" button at the bottom of the screen.

When you shut off your phone, you won't receive texts, calls, alerts, or revive any notifications. It is almost like your phone is "temporarily dead".

To power your phone back on, you can just hold the power button down until the glowing Apple logo comes up.

If you press and hold the power button to power on your phone, but your phone's battery is dead, you will be shown an icon with a battery that is empty. You will have to plug your phone into a charger if you want to continue using your phone at this point.

THE EMERGENCY SOS FEATURE

iPhones have a way to easily call emergency services if you need to. There are two different ways of activating Emergency SOS:

1. If you hold down the power button and one of the volume buttons, one of the options that you are given, is for "Emergency SOS". You can swipe right on this, and it will begin to call the emergency service for your correct location (depending got where you live).

2. The other way, is if you continue to hold down the power button and volume buttons, but instead of stopping when the prompts appear, you continue to hold them down. After a couple of seconds, a countdown sequence will begin, and your phone will start to make noise.

Congratulations! You made it through this chapter! These gestures that you have learned in this chapter are the fundamentals of working your new iPhone. I hope that it was fun to play with them, and that you weren't too frustrated!

If you want more practice using the gestures explained in this chapter, feel free to jump back to sections, re-read them, and practice some more! Practice makes perfect, and practice is key to fluency on your new phone!

CHAPTER TEN

YOUR HOME SCREEN

When you unlock your phone, you should be greeted with a nice grid of apps. It should look like this:

This is where all of your apps "live". If you want to open a certain app, you must return to your home screen first. In this chapter, we will talk about the different aspects of the home screen.

YOUR HOME SCREEN HAS 'PAGES'

On your home screen, there are a couple of different 'pages' of apps. You can swipe left and right on your phone to go from page to page. Your phone will most likely have three pages if you are setting it up for the first time. The pages are indicated by a series of dots towards the bottom of the screen:

One dot represents one page. The highlighted dot (the bright white one) is the page that you are currently on.

Note: Your phone will typically have three pages after you set it up for the first time. Because I have had my phone for a while, I have downloaded a bunch of other apps that have required additional pages on my home screen. We will learn about how to download additional apps towards the end of this book.

Here is something confusing though; the image above says that we are on page two. Page one is a little unique. Page one has something called widgets on them. This is what they look like:

| Page 1 | Page 2 | Page 3 |

Usually, the first page isn't looked at that much. You can think of page one like a "widget page"; it is the only page that doesn't have any apps on it. This is why it is unique from the others.

THE DOCK

The dock is the bottom area of the home screen. This is what it looks like:

When you switch pages on the home screen, these apps stay in place. The four apps in the dock are "locked" there; every page of the home screen will have the same four apps in the dock. People usually put their favorite or most used apps in the dock for easy access. We will learn about how to re-arrange apps later so you can change the apps in your dock if you wish to.

APPLE'S STOCK APPS

When you first set up your phone, your phone will have pre-installed Apple apps on your home screen. They are all made by Apple. They are super useful, and you can get a lot out of your phone by only using these apps. I will briefly talk about what these apps are and how you can use them now. We will go into more detail later about certain apps in the following chapters.

 Starting on the dock, this app is simply called Phone. This is the app that you would use to call people.

 This is Safari. This is the app that you use if you want to look something up on the internet.

 This is Messages. You use this app to text people.

 This is Music. This is Apple's default app for listening to music!

 This is FaceTime. This app allows you to video-chat people (almost like calling, but you can see the other person on your screen).

 This is Calendar. In this app, you can enter in dates, events, and other important things to remember!

 This is Photos. In this app, you can view all of the photos and videos that are saved to your device.

 This is Camera. In this app, you can take pictures and record videos straight to your phone!

This is Mail. With this app, you can send and receive emails straight from your iPhone! Pretty cool, right?

 This is Clock. In this app, you can set alarms and use things like stopwatches and timers!

 This is Maps. This app is used for GPS and getting from point A to point B!

 This is Weather. In this app, you can view the weather in your area, or the weather in other places around the world!

 This is Reminders. In this app, you can set reminders for yourself!

 This is Notes. In this app, you can take notes (using your phone's on-screen keyboard).

 This is Stocks. In this app, you can analyze and keep track of stocks.

 This is News. In this app, you can subscribe to different news outlets and get notified when they post a new story.

 This is Books. In this app, you can download and read e-books on your phone!

 This is the App Store. This is the app that you will use to purchase other apps for your use!

This is Podcasts. In this app, you can listen to podcasts.

 This is TV. TV is Apple's TV streaming service that you can use to watch TV shows.

 This is Health. In this app, you can set it up so your phone tracks some of your health data (like steps, distance traveled, etc.)

 This is Home. If you have smart-home devices, you can control them using this app, straight from your phone.

 This is Wallet. If you want to add your credit or debit card to your phone to use Apple Pay, this is where your cards are stored. I will talk more about how to set Apple Pay up and use it to make purchases, in a later chapter.

 This is Settings. In this app, you can truly customize your phone and make it yours. We will talk a lot about settings at the end of the book.

 This is Files. In this app, you can view some of the files (like documents and stuff) on your phone.

 This app is Find My iPhone. If someone else looses their phone, they can use this app (on your phone) to find it.

 This is the iTunes Store. This is the app where you can buy music, to listen to in the Music app.

This is the Tips app. If you want to learn more about your phone after reading this book, you can check out this app to a learn a couple neat tricks and tips.

This is Contacts. You will use this app to create contacts for other people to call, text, or interact with.

This is Watch. You will use this app if you have an Apple Watch and would like to pair it with your phone. If you do not have an Apple Watch or don't plan on getting one, you can ignore this app or delete it later.

This is a folder. Just like how you can store multiple things in a real folder, these folders store multiple apps in one spot. You can use folders to group a couple of different apps together.

This is Voice Memos. If you would like to record a voice memo, this is the app that you will use. It is relatively simple, and simply records your voice so that you can listen to it later.

This is Compass. In this app, you can use a compass.

This is Measure. In this app, you can do two things; (1) Measure things using AR Kit, or (2) use a leveler.

The last app, is Calculator. This works the exact same way as a regular calculator. Heres an interesting tip: if you rotate your phone (with orientation-lock off), then you will be able to use extra functions on the calculator.

NOTIFICATION BADGES

On some of your app icons, you may see a red dot in the top right corner of the app with a number inscribed in it. The number inside of the red dot tells you how many notifications that you have for that specific app.

The mail app here, has 144 notifications (in this case, unread emails).

THE APP LIBRARY PAGE

When Apple released iOS 14, they added a new feature called the App Library. (If you have iOS 13 or newer, then this feature will not be on your phone!)

If you look back to page 90, you will see that I mentioned how your iPhone has a couple of different "pages". But I didn't tell you everything. While exploring your phone, or viewing the different pages on your home screen, you may have noticed that there is an additional, unmarked page that has a gridded-list of all of the apps that you have downloaded on your phone.

> Note: If you are having trouble finding the App Library "page" on your phone's home screen, you can continually swipe left (while on your home screen) until it slides onto your phone's screen!

This is what it looks like:

Basically, what the App Library is, is a library of all your apps. Similarly to how a real library works, this interface allows you to view all of the apps that you have on your phone. Your phone intelligently indexes the apps that you have, and sorts them into pre-made categories that can help you find them easier (almost like a built-in librarian, if you ask me!)

You can click into the categories of apps to see additional apps that might also be apart of this category too, by clicking on the four apps icons that are smaller than the rest of the other apps in that category (look in the bottom right corner of each category square).

You can also use the search bar function, found at the top of the App Library, to quickly find and access apps that you are looking for. If you click on the search bar at the top, you can also view all of your apps in alphabetical order for easy searching!

Although the App Library feature isn't one used that often, it is nice to know about it incase you need it!

CHAPTER ELEVEN

EXPLORING, CREATING, AND EDITING YOUR CONTACTS

Before we learn how to call or text anyone, we have to learn how to create contacts for your family and friends.

Now, you may be thinking, "I have to remember everyone's phone number? How is that possible?" Luckily for you, your phone remembers all of them for you, inside of the Contacts app. This is kind of like an interactive phone book.

We will now begin to explore the Contacts app. First, let's open the Contacts app. This is what it looks like:

The Contacts app is relatively simple, in the sense that it only has one tab. This is what it looks like:

Because this is my personal phone, I have my own contacts in here (I have blurred them out). Your contact list might be blank at the moment, or you might have one or two contacts in here if a family member has added them in for you.

First, let's learn about how to create a new contact.

CREATING A NEW CONTACT

To create a new contact, first click the "+" icon in the top right corner. This will bring up the screen in which you will have to input the information about the person who you are making this contact for (there is an image on the next page).

You can fill this information out in any order that you would like to. The only things that you really really need from the person, is their name and their cell-phone number. If you would like to fill out their email, home-phone, and address, you can do that too.

Once you have all of the person's information filled in, you can click "Done" in the top right corner. Congrats! You've created your first contact! Now their number (and any other information that you might have put in), is saved on your device forever!

> Tip: You can also add a photo to the person's contact, by clicking on the large gray circle (with the little person in it) at the top of the screen (it also says "Add Photo" below it). This will prompt you to choose a photo from the photos saved on your device, or to take a photo of the person right now.

EXPLORING CONTACT CARDS

Contact cards are little digital cards that have all of the information that you entered in about the person when you originally made their contact. If you are looking at the list of all of your contacts, (like the picture on page 100), and you can click on one of the names in the list, then that person's contact card will appear. It may look like this:

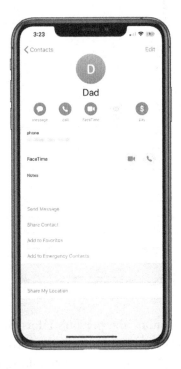

The image above is the contact card for my dad. On my dad's contact card, you can see the information that I have entered in for him when originally created his contact card years ago. The only piece of information that I have in there, is his phone number (I have blurred it out). If you look above his blurred out phone number, you can see a myriad of options in little circles:

We will learn about what each of these buttons do later.

EDITING SOMEONE'S CONTACT

When my dad got a new phone number a couple of weeks ago, I had to edit his contact card and change the number (because his new phone came with a new phone number).

To edit someone's contact, you first have to open their contact card.

Do you see the edit button on the top right corner (there is a picture on the left)? If you click the edit button, the information on the contact card becomes editable, and you can change some of the information on it, by tapping on the pieces that you wish to change. You can also add new information to the person's contact card if you wish. This is what editing a contact card looks like:

After you make changes, make sure you hit the "Done" button on the top of the screen. This will save any of the changes that you make. If you decide that you aren't going to make any changes, you can press the "Cancel" button.

CHAPTER TWELVE

CALLING YOUR LOVED ONES

One of the most important functions of your phone is calling somebody. If you have grandkids (unfortunately, no, I am not one of your grandkids; it's pretty sad, I know), they will be so psyched to hear from you! Calling someone is super simple and easy to do. This is what the Phone app looks like:

If you click on the app to open it, you should be launched into the Phone app. If you look towards the bottom of the phone's screen, you will see the five different "tabs" of this app:

These five tabs are favorites, recents, contacts, keypad, and voicemail. Let's go through what each tab is, and what you can do on each of them. To switch tabs, simply click on the tab's icon. When it is selected, the tab icon should turn blue.

THE KEYPAD

Let's start with the Keypad tab. Click on the keypad icon. This screen should now be shown on your phone:

This tab in the phone app allows you to dial any phone number that you wish. You can just click on the numbered buttons, and the number that you just dialed should show up in the blank space above the keypad. Once you start typing a phone number, a little backspace icon will show up below the '#' symbol. It looks like this:

If you make a mistake while typing a phone number, you can click this backspace button, and it will delete the number that you had just mistakenly pressed.

Once you've finished typing in the number, you can click the green call button towards the bottom of the screen. This will dial their phone, and you will be shown the calling interface (which is described in a couple of pages).

Now, let's move on to another tab.

CALL PEOPLE IN YOUR CONTACTS

Click onto the contacts tab. Your screen should look like this:

You may be thinking that this page looks similar to the Contacts app. It actually works the same way too.

Let's call someone. For demonstration purposes, I will call my dad. I will first scroll down until I find his contact. It is under "Dad", so I will look for that. Next, I will click on his name. This will open his contact card:

If we look closely at the buttons below my dad's name, we can see that one of them is a button to call him. I have circled it below:

Once you click call, you should now be met with the calling interface. We will talk about the calling interface at the end of this chapter.

> Tip: Because the same options in the picture above are shown in the Contact app (on the person's contact card), you can also call people directly from the Contacts app by clicking that same icon.

YOUR RECENT CALLS

Let's move onto another tab in the phone app. Click the recent tab. You should see this screen now:

Here, you can see a list of all of your recent calls. Because we just called my dad, he is shown at the top of the list.

> Tip: The cool thing about this page, is that if we click on my dad's name, it will re-dial his phone number. This is a quick and easy shortcut if you call the same people often.

YOUR FAVORITE PEOPLE DESERVE THEIR OWN PLACE

Let's move onto another tab. Click the favorites icon. You should be met with this screen:

Here, you can add people to your favorites list, like your family members or best friends. This makes it easy to call them quickly. If you want to add someone to your favorites list, you can click the "+" button on the top left corner. Once there are people in your favorites list, you can simply click on their name to call them (just like how you would in the Recent tab).

VOICEMAILS

When other people call you, they might leave a voicemail. If they do, you will be able to find these voicemails in the voicemail tab on the bottom of the screen. This is the last tab of the phone app. If you click on it, you should see a screen that looks like this:

Here, we can see that I have one voicemail from my mom. If we were to click on her name to view the voicemail, we would see this screen:

To listen to the voicemail, you can hit the play button. After you listen to it, you can also delete it using the trash-can icon on the right side of the screen. You can also hit the phone icon button to return a call to them if you would like to.

THE CALLING INTERFACE

When you use any of the methods to call someone, you will be met with the calling interface. It looks like this:

There are only three main buttons that we have to worry about here.

1. The end call button: If you press the big red end-call button at the bottom of your screen, you will end the call (ending the call is also known as hanging-up).

2. The mute button: if you click the mute button, it will mute your microphone, and the other person will not be able to hear what you are saying. If you click it again, it will unmute your microphone.

3. The keypad button. If you click the keypad button, the keypad will pop up again. You might need this in situations where you have to dial an extension number to reach a certain person.

WHAT TO DO WHEN SOMEONE IS CALLING YOU

When someone is calling you, this will pop up on your screen:

If you wish to accept their call, you can hit "Accept". If you wish to decline their call, you can hit "Decline". Declining the call will send the other person straight to your voicemail.

When someone is calling you, your phone will ring and make noise (unless you have your ring switch set to silent mode, in which it will just vibrate instead).

Note: When someone calls you, your phone will ring and make noise if you are in ring mode. If you are in silent mode, your phone will vibrate a couple of times. To switch back and forth between ring mode and silent mode, you have to use the ring switch. To learn more about the ring switch, you can go back to page 66.

Tip: Here is an advanced tip that not many people know about: If you don't want to hit decline or accept for a call that you are receiving, your phone will continue to ring until they reach your voicemail. If you do not want to hear the ringing or vibrating noises, you can hit the power button once, and it will silence the call. Your phone will stop ringing or vibrating. However, the call interface will still be shown, and the person will still be "calling" you. Silencing the call merely just stops the ringing or vibrating from happening.

The phone app is relatively simple, and as you may have realized, there are a lot of different ways to do the same thing. It's all about picking the method that you want to use.

CHAPTER THIRTEEN

TEXTING PEOPLE

In this chapter, you are going to learn how to start a new conversation with someone and send them text messages. Texting is done in the Messages app.

The Messages app looks like this:

When you click on it to open it, you will be greeted with this screen:

This screen will show all of the conversations that you are having with other people.

STARTING A NEW CONVERSATION

To start a new conversation on your iPhone, press the "new conversation" button in the top right corner. It looks like this:

Once you click this button, you will be prompted to type in the name of the person that you want to create the conversation with.

> Note: If you type a person's name into this text box, the person has to be a contact on your phone. If the person you want to text isn't in your contacts, you can also just type their phone number into this spot.

Write the name of the recipient of your text in here.

Write your message here. This is the text messaging field.

When this screen pops up, your cursor will already be in the text field where you will write the name of the contact that you want to send the message to.

After you write the recipients name, you can begin to write your message. To change the placement of your cursor, you can tap in the text messaging field. When you finish typing your message, you can send it. This is what the send button looks like:

Now your message is sent!

The next time that you want to text this same person, you do not have to create a new conversation. Instead, you can scroll through the list of conversations that first appear when you open the app. When you look at this list of conversations and find the specific conversation that you want to view, you can click on it and the conversation will open up.

WHAT ARE READ RECEIPTS?

When you first open the Messages app, you might be asked if you would like to turn "Read Receipts" on. Read receipts are something that you can turn on, and alert the other person in the conversation that you read a message that they sent. In the picture below, you can see a conversation in which my mom had her read receipts on, and I was alerted that she read my message. It looks like this:

When the phone asks if you want to turn on read receipts, they are asking if you want others to know when you read their message.

WHY ARE MY TEXT MESSAGE BUBBLES DIFFERENT COLORS?

In the Messages app, there are two different colors that your messages can be. If the message bubbles that you send are blue, then that means that the recipient of the text also has an iPhone. However, if the messages that you are sending someone are green, then this person doesn't have an iPhone (they might have an android, or another type of phone).

DELETING CONVERSATIONS

In the future, you might want to delete a conversation. If you want to do so, you can swipe left on the conversation (in the conversation list view), and click "Delete". It will have you confirm that you want to delete it, and you can either confirm it (by clicking "Delete") or cancel it.

GROUP MESSAGES

There might be a time where you are included in a group message, or you would like to create one. Group messages are conversations that have multiple people in them. Here is an example of a group message between my mom, my dad, and me:

You can tell who wrote the message, by looking at the name above the bubble (the messages that are sent by me, are shown on the right side of the screen, while the messages sent by everybody else are shown on the left side of the screen).

Group messages are a nice and easy way to message multiple people at once. But how do we create a group message? It is easy! You can use the same process to create a group message as the one you use when you create a regular conversation with just one person. This time, for a group message, just add multiple names into the "To;" text box where you enter the recipient's names.

VIEWING AND SAVING IMAGES

Occasionally, someone might send you an image through text. If this is the case, you might want to save the photo to your device. When you save a photo to your device, it ends up in the Photos app. We will learn more about the Photos app later.

Let's learn about saving a photo, through an example. Let's say that my dad sent me a photo. It would look like this on my screen:

If you want to view the picture better, or enlarge it, you can tap on it. Once you do this, you can zoom in, zoom out, or just examine the photo. This is what the enlarged view looks like:

When you are done looking at the photo, you can hit the "done" button in the top left corner, and you will return back to the conversation.

When you are looking at the image in the conversation view (not enlarged), you can long press on the image, and you will get three options of things that you can do with the image:

These options are copy, save, and more. If you want to save the photo to the Photos app, you can press "Save".

The "Copy" button, would copy it to your clipboard, and you can "Paste" it somewhere else. This is kind of like ctrl-c and ctrl-v (copy and paste), which you might have learned about when using a computer.

The "More" button is kind of pointless. Let me explain. If you click the "More" button, then it will allow you to delete the image from this conversation. Once you click the button, the interface will change, and you will see a little check mark next to the image. This check mark means that the image is selected. If you click on the checkmark, you can deselect the image, and the check mark will turn into an empty circle. You may notice that other messages might have empty circles next to them too. If you click on the empty circle, a check mark will appear. If you ever want to delete a message, this is how you would go about it. You might also see a "Delete All" button in the left corner of your phone. If you click this while images or messages are selected, then they will be deleted.

Deleting messages definitely isn't necessary, and I don't think I've ever deleted one specific message before.

One thing to keep in mind too, is that if you delete a certain message, it only deletes it off of your phone. This means that it will still show up on the other person's phone. For this reason, deleting messages is kinda pointless. Because it is kinda pointless, I am not making a whole section about it. But, that is what the "More" button does, if you are curious.

HOW DO I SEND PICTURES TO SOMEONE?

We will talk more about sending photos and videos to other people when we talk about the Photos app later in this book!

DICTATING MESSAGES

Your phone comes with this really cool feature, where it will type the things that you say. I know, it sounds like it is straight out of a sci-fi movie. If you want to dictate a text message, you can click the little microphone button in the bottom right corner of your keyboard:

Your keyboard will change, and it will look like this:

Now, you can start talking, and your phone will start to type the things that you say. When you are done speaking, you can tap the little keyboard icon at the bottom of your screen. This will return you back to your keyboard.

RESPONDING TO MESSAGES FROM THE LOCKSCREEN

When you get a message notification on your lock screen, there is an easy way to reply to it without having to unlock your phone and opening the Messages app. Here is what a message notification looks like on the lockscreen:

If I wanted to reply to it straight from the lockscreen, I can long-press on the notification box itself. The notification box will expand, and a keyboard will pop up, and allow you to type a quick message back to the person who sent the text. This is what it looks like:

When you are done, you can click the "X" in the top right corner, the notification box will disappear, and you will be back at your lockscreen.

Using this method to respond quickly to text messages saves some time!

EMOJIS

Emojis are pretty much second nature when you are texting someone. Personally, I use them in about 50% of the texts that I send. If you want to text an emoji, you can click the emoji button on the bottom left corner of the keyboard. This is what the button looks like:

Once you click this button, your keyboard will change, and will be replaced by a bunch of different colored icons; these are called emojis. You can scroll left and right to view additional emojis.

If you want to send an emoji, all you have to do is press the emoji that you wish to type. When you are satisfied, you can hit the ABC button (in the same location as the emoji button), and you will return back to the keyboard.

REACTIONS

Reactions is a feature that was introduced to iMessage a couple of years ago. It is a way of quickly reacting to something using icons, instead of actual words. If you want to use the "reactions", you can press and hold on a message, and the reactions will pop up above the message.

You may be familiar with the "Copy", and "More" buttons, but right now we are looking at the six icons that are shown above the message. You might have noticed them when we were talking about saving a photo. Anyways, these six icons are known as the "reactions". If you would like to use one of them, just click the one that you wish to send. For example, because this person got his promotion, I would click the thumbs-up icon, or maybe the exclamation marks. This is what the thumbs-up reaction looks like after I click it:

This is another feature that I don't use too often, but it is cool to play around with! Im sure your family members would be super duper impressed if you sent them one of the reactions!

THE APP DRAWER

This section will be confusing, and quite complicated. Make sure that you are familiar with the rest of the Messages app and the things we covered in this chapter before you read this last section.

The app drawer is a section of your screen, that is shown right above your keyboard. It looks like this:

Here, you can do different tasks and interact with messages in other ways besides texting. For example you can send stickers, play iMessage games (we will talk about iMessage games later), and bunch of other things.

In the most simplistic way of saying it, the app drawer can give you quick access to some of the apps on your phone that send content through iMessage.

For example, the Photos app in the app drawer gives you quick access to sending photos. There are two methods of sending photos through iMessage. The first way can be done by using the Photos app in the app drawer. This is what the Photos app in the app drawer looks like:

If you click this on this button, some of your recent photos will be shown in the space where you keyboard used to be. If you want to send one of the photos shown here, you can simply tap on it. The photo will then appear in the text field, and you can send it. Again, this is one way of sending photos through iMessage, and we will talk about the other way when we talk about the Photos app.

The next icon, is the Apple Pay icon. Here, you can send and receive payments to and from other people all through your conversation in Messages. I will talk more about Apple Pay and how to set it all up in a later chapter.

The next icon we will talk about, is the "#images" icon. This is what it looks like:

#images is an app in the app drawer where you can send GIFs, or moving images. If you click on this icon, the keyboard will be replaced with a grid go GIFs that you can choose to send. Here is an example of what it might look like:

Note: In the image on the previous page, I showed empty GIF slots. On your phone, you will have GIFs where the empty spots are.

You can also use the search bar, to search for relevant GIFs that you would like to send. For example, if you wanted to send a GIF of someone dancing, you could type "dancing" into this search bar.

GIFs are fun, and make the conversation more fun too. Your family members will be super impressed if you send a GIF to them through iMessage. Pat yourself on the back if you are able send GIFs; it is extremely difficult!

The next icon we will talk about is Memoji. This is what the icon looks like:

This app in the app drawer is only available on certain devices. In this app, you can customize a little emoji-version of yourself.

If you click on it for the first time, your phone will walk you through the steps to create a Memoji. Once you have finished creating one, you will be able to use them in your conversations within the Messages app. This is what my Memoji look like:

If you want to send one of them, all you have to do is tap the one you wish to send, and it will insert itself into the text field. Then, you can use the send button to deliver your message to the recipient.

The next icon we will talk about, is Animoji. Animoji is similar to the Memojis, except for the fact that Animojis are the animated versions of the Memojis. Animoji is only available on the devices that have Face ID. The Animoji app in the app drawer looks like this:

Once you click on this app in the app drawer, it will bring up this screen where the keyboard used to be:

If you hold your phone parallel to your face, you can see that the Animoji (for me it was a monkey), moves and reacts to your facial expressions. Try it out! Make some goofy faces, and see how the Animoji reacts!

You can also swipe horizontally on the screen to switch between different animals. It's quite a lot of fun to play with!

The last thing that we are going to talk about, is how you would add apps to this app drawer. To do this, we will use the app store that can be found in the app drawer. This is what it looks like:

In the app store inside of the app drawer, you can buy things like sticker packs, or iMessage games, which are little games that you can play with people through iMessage.

iMessage games are super fun, and they are a nice way to play a game with someone else over text. Most people (like maybe your grandchildren) already have iMessage games installed on their phones.

WRAPPING UP THIS CHAPTER...

Now that we have explored the Messages app, you should be feeling pretty confident about it. If you are nervous about the app drawer, or feel less confident about it, thats totally okay. The app drawer is complicated, and honestly, isn't used that often. But, it is nice to know about if you would like to explore it for yourself!

The best way to practice texting, using the keyboard, and other features of the Messages app, is to send messages! Start texting your family and friends; they will love to hear from you!

CHAPTER FOURTEEN

FACE TIME; A BETTER WAY TO CONNECT

In the past three chapters, you have learned about the basic functions of you phone; calling, texting, and adding contacts to your phone.

The next thing that we will learn about, is FaceTime. FaceTime is super easy way to video chat your friends or family. It is similar to calling somebody; the only difference being that you are able to see the person while you talk. It is so much more fun than calling; there is just something special about it.

When my grandmother first got her iPhone, she didn't tell me about it right away. Instead, she FaceTimed me. This shocked me. I was looking at the name that the FaceTime call was coming from, and I couldn't believe that it was my grandmother. I was so psyched for her, and excited that we would be able to talk face-to-face easier (she lives far away, so it is hard to see each other in person). I think that your family members or friends will have a similar reaction when you FaceTime them.

Before we get started, we have to talk about a caveat of FaceTime. FaceTime only works if the other person has an iPhone. In other words, you cannot FaceTime someone that doesn't have an iPhone. Luckily for you, most people have iPhones.

Let's gets started. This is what the FaceTime app looks like:

When you open the app, it should look like this:

Just like we did in the Messages app, we will have to hit the "+" button on the top right of the screen to begin our first call. Once we hit the button, we will be prompted to enter in the person's name.

Note: If you type a person's name into this text box, the person has to be a contact on your phone. If the person you want to text isn't in your contacts, you can also just type their phone number into this spot.

Note: If a person does not have an iPhone, then you will not be able to FaceTime them. If this is the case, then person's name (that doesn't have the iPhone) will be grayed out, and you will not be able to click on it.

Once you type someone's name and select it from the list of search results that pop up, you will be given two options just above your keyboard. It will look like this:

These two options are either FaceTime Audio, or FaceTime Video. The buttons do exactly what you would think they would do:

FaceTime Audio doesn't show your face to the other person when you call them. You might be thinking, "Isn't that the same thing as calling someone?" and you would be correct for thinking this. There is one key reason that you would use FaceTime Audio instead of calling someone regularly, and it is if you don't have signal. If your phone says "NO SIGNAL" in the status bar on the top of your phone, and you are still connected to WiFi or have a cellular connection, then you can use FaceTime Audio. Let me give you an example of where this would possibly come into play: In my house, my room is in our finished basement. Because it is in the basement, sometimes I don't have signal, or enough of a connection to make a call. For this reason, I would use FaceTime Audio, because I am still connected to WiFi. Other than this, I don't really use FaceTime Audio that much.

The other option, is FaceTime Video. When people say, "Lets FaceTime," they are typically going to use FaceTime Video. This is the option that we will talk about in the rest of this chapter.

Let's make a FaceTime Video call. You can click this button:

Once you click that button, your FaceTime call will start ringing. This is what it should look like:

When the other person picks up your call, the interface changes, and the FaceTime call interface should show up. You can see the other person's face in the middle of your screen. You can also see your own face in its own little box, in the top right hand corner.

Here is what my phone's screen would look like. Because this is my phone's screen, I can see what I look like in the top right corner. My dad (waving) is what is the large figure that takes up the whole screen.

Here is what my dad's phone would look like. He sees me taking up the whole screen, while he sees himself in the top right corner.

In the example pictures above, I am showing what my phone (the one on the left) and my dad's phone (on the right) would look like during a FaceTime call.

FACETIME ON SCREEN CONTROLS

During a FaceTime call, you can view the on screen controls at the bottom of the screen. This is what they look like:

We will talk about what the buttons do, but first let's talk about how you can hide/show the on screen controls.

The on screen controls take up a pretty decent amount of space at the bottom of your screen. If you would like to hide them, you can tap in the middle of your screen, and they will go away. If you would like to bring them back, you can simply tap in the middle of your screen again.

Now, lets talk about the toggles that can be found on the on screen controls:

This is the mute button. You can press it to toggle your microphone on and off. This works the same as the "Mute" button that you can see when you are making a phone call.

This is the flip camera button. This flips your cameras from your front-facing camera, to your back-facing camera. This is a convenient way to show something that is in front of you to the person that you are on FaceTime with.

Lastly, this is the button you would press if you would like to end the call.

YOUR RECENT FACETIME CALLS

Once you (or the other person) ends the call, you may notice that you see their name on the original FaceTime screen, like this:

This works the same as your recent calls in the Phone app. In the future, if you would like to FaceTime someone that you have already FaceTimed with in the past, you can simply click their name in this list (instead of clicking the "+" button to start a new call). This will re-dial them!

GROUP FACETIME CALLS

A couple of years ago, Apple released a new feature that allowed group FaceTime (multiple people FaceTiming at once). This is what the interface will look like for group FaceTime:

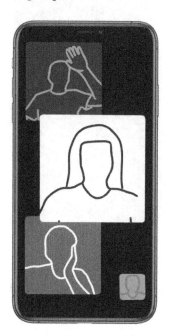

There are two ways to start a group FaceTime call. The first way to start a group FaceTime call, is to type two or more names when you click the "+":

The second way to initiate a group FaceTime call, is to add someone to a FaceTime call that you are already in. To do this, you first have to swipe up on the on-screen controls at the bottom of your screen. This will expand the on-screen controls:

Now, you can click the "Add Person" button. This will bring up a text box in which you can add another person to the call.

When you have more than two people in a group FaceTime call, the other people will show up in square tiles. These tiles will increase in size when a person is speaking (when a person isn't speaking, their square tile will be smaller than the rest). This is a neat way to see who is talking during a conversation.

That is everything you need to know about FaceTime! FaceTime is really neat, and it is a nice way to talk to people. I highly recommend you try FaceTime out with your family and friends; you won't regret it!

CHAPTER FIFTEEN

"LOOKING THINGS UP"

Arguably one of the most used features on smart phones, is the ability to look things up. On your iPhone, there is already an app installed that will allow you to do this! It is called Safari, and it looks like this:

This is what Safari looks like when you first open it:

If you want to look something up, you can simply type the thing that you are looking for into the search bar at the top. If there is a specific website that you would like to look up, you can also type it in here. Once you click on the search bar, your keyboard will pop up. After you type what you want to search for into the search bar, you can click the blue "go" button in the bottom right corner of your phone's keyboard. It looks like this:

Once you hit "go", search results will start to pop up on the screen. You can scroll up and down to look at the different results. If you have searched for something on the internet using a computer, searching for something using Safari will be a similar process.

Once you find a website that you like or would like to check out, you can simply click on the blue headline of that website. This will redirect you to the webpage that you clicked on. Here, you can explore, read, and learn whatever you'd like to from the webpage.

You might notice certain buttons on the bottom of your screen:

Each of these buttons do their own thing. Let's go through them now.

This is the "back" button. If you have clicked on a search result's headline and opened up a webpage, but you later want to return back to the list of search results, you would click this.

This is the forward button. If you ever accidentally click the "back" button, or wish to go back to the screen that you were at before you hit the "back" button, you can click this button.

This is the share button. You would click this if you want to share a webpage with someone. Clicking this button brings up the share card, where you can chose how you would like to share it. For example, you can text it to someone by clicking on the Messages app icon that is shown on the share card. (There is an image of what the share card looks like on the next page).

This is the button where you can access your bookmarks, reading list, or browsing history. Personally, I don't use this button that much.

This is the button that you can press to view all of the tabs that you have open on your phone. This button isn't used that often. If you click it, the interface will change a little bit. At the top left of the webpage you were looking at, you can see a little "X". If you click this, it will quit the webpage. This will the close the webpage indefinitely. In this new interface, you might also notice a "+" centered at the very bottom of your screen. This will add a new tab to Safari where you can search for something else. I would recommend quitting all of your Safari tabs every once in a while to keep your phone fast and fresh!

SHARING WEBPAGES WITH SOMEONE ELSE

Although this action probably won't be on the list of "Top Actions You Do on Your Phone," it is necessary to learn how to do this to introduce other topics.

To share a webpage with someone else, first click the share button (review the icons on the page before if you forget what the share button looks like). Once you click the share button, the share card will pop up:

The share card is a little screen that will pop up every time you want to share something; it will look relatively the same every time, regardless of what you are sharing.

Let's demonstrate how to share something through an example: Let's say you wanted to share this webpage to someone else through text (which is probably the way that you are going to share webpages, pictures, etc. the most). Once the share card is up, you can simply tap the Messages icon. Then, it will prompt you to enter in the name of the person you wish to send this webpage to. After you do that, you can click the send button.

YOUR FAVORITE WEBPAGES

If you have a certain webpage that you use often, or would like to have easy access to (without having to search for it every time you want to view it), you can add it to your favorites list.

To add a webpage to your favorites list, you first have to open the share card. If you scroll up to expand the share card, you will see a myriad of options to choose from.

This is what the expanded version of the share card looks like:

If you want to add a webpage to your favorites list, you can simply click "Add to Favorites".

Now we will talk about how to view all of the websites that you have favorited. There are two places where your favorite webpages can be viewed.

The first place that your favorite webpages are shown, is every time you go to search for something. When you click in the search bar, your favorite webpages are shown underneath the search bar. It looks like this:

If you add webpages to your favorites list, this is where they will appear.

The other place where your favorite webpages are shown, is when you create a new tab. Review the ⬜ symbol to learn how to access all of your tabs, and how to create a new tab. Here is what your favorite webpages look like when they are found on a new tab:

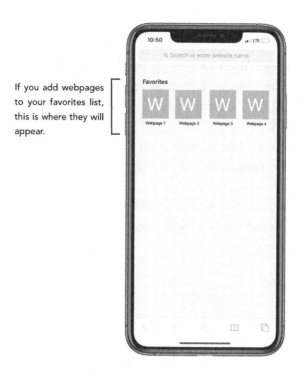

If you add webpages to your favorites list, this is where they will appear.

To visit one of your favorite webpages, all you have to do is click on the icon of the webpage that you wish to visit.

SAVING PHOTOS FROM THE INTERNET

Sometimes, you might want to save an image from the internet to send to someone, or to just keep for yourself. In order to look at images for the things that you search for, you will have to switch to the "images" tab that shows up at the very top of the search results (after you already search for something). To do this, you can tap the "images" button that is found below the search bar.

In the example above, I searched for carrots. To see pictures of carrots, I will select the "Images" tab. Safari will reload, and pictures of carrots will pop up. You can also explore the other tabs like shopping, news, videos, maps, books, etc (these tabs don't make much sense for carrots, but you can imagine how those tabs would apply to other relevant searches).

If you would like to enlarge an image to see it clearly, you can simply tap on the image you wish to enlarge. This will make the picture fill your screen.

Now, if you'd like to save an image, you first have to enlarge it. Next, if you press and hold on the image, these options will pop up:

If you wish to save the photo to your Photos app, you can click "Add to Photos". If you press the "Share" button, the share card (page 150) will pop up, and you can share the image through Messages, or other apps that pop up in the share card. You can also press "Copy", which will copy the image to your clipboard. If you copy something to your clipboard, you can then paste the thing that you've copied some-where else (like in a text field).

To "Paste" something that is copied to your clipboard, you have to press and hold inside of a text-box. Once you press and hold in a text-box you will be given the option to paste the thing that you've copied:

CHAPTER SIXTEEN

iPHONE PHOTOGRAPHY PART 1: THE CAMERA APP

The cameras on mobile devices are so good and so powerful. You can capture extremely nice images with the camera right on your phone.

Before we start, let's examine the cameras that you have on the outside of your device. If you look on the back of your phone, you may see one of these five camera configurations:

Within the five different camera configurations, there are three different types of cameras that you could possibly have; the standard camera, telephoto (zoomed-in) camera, and the wide-angle camera. The reason that you might want to switch between the different cameras, is just for a different look for your photo. Here is what the three cameras would look like if you were to take a picture with each of them:

This is what the standard camera would look like.

This is what the telephoto (zoomed-in) camera would look like.

This is what the wide-angle camera would look like.

The standard camera is definitely used nine times out of ten, but the other cameras might come in handy at some point. Here is how you can tell which of the three cameras you have on your phone:

If your phone has this type of camera configuration on the back, then you have one single camera, and it is the standard camera.

If your phone has this type of camera layout on the back, then you have two cameras; one standard and one telephoto camera.

If your phone has this type of camera layout on the back, then you also have two cameras; one standard and one telephoto camera.

If your phone has this type of camera layout on the back, then you have one standard camera and one wide-angle camera.

If your phone has this type of camera layout on the back, then you have all three cameras; one standard camera, one telephoto camera, and one wide-angle camera.

We will learn how to switch between the different cameras (the ones that you have) a little bit later, but it is important to note how many cameras that you have on the back of your phone.

Let's first begin by talking about the Camera app. The Camera app allows you to take pictures and record videos. These photos and videos that you take will be automatically saved to your Photos app. We will talk about the photos app in the next chapter.

The camera app looks like this:

When you first open the app, you will be greeted with a screen that looks like this:

This is what the main camera screen looks like. There are a lot of buttons, I know, but we will go through them individually.

Lets start at the bottom of the screen:

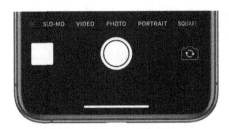

The main button that you need to know, is the big white circular shutter button. When you click this, your phone will take a picture.

You will know if you've taken a picture, when you see a thumbnail of the photo that you just took, in the photos preview box that can be found to the left of the shutter button. This little box shows the most recent picture that you've taken on your phone. Therefore, you'll know when you've taken a photo, when you see it appear in this box.

To the right of the shutter button, is the camera-flip button. Just like how it works in FaceTime, this will flip your camera between front-facing and back-facing. This is convenient if you would like to switch between taking selfies and taking landscape photos.

Just above the shutter button, you will see a bunch of words like video, photo, portrait, etc. This is the mode-wheel. It tells you which camera mode you are in. When you first open the camera app, you will be in the default 'photo' mode. To switch modes, you can swipe left or right on the camera screen.

Next, we will talk about the different camera modes.

PHOTO MODE

Photo mode is the most basic camera mode, and the mode that you will probably use 99.9% of the time!

When you want to take a regular photo, you will use photo mode. Just like we learned before, to take a photo we can click the white circular shutter button.

Your phone's camera will autofocus for you. It will pick what it thinks is the subject of the photo, and focus on it. However, sometimes it doesn't get it right and you might have to do it for yourself. If you have to focus the camera for yourself, you can tap on the subject you want the camera to focus on. This little icon should show up on the screen where you just tapped:

Another reason that you might want to tap to focus, is if your subject is too dark or too light. Let me explain this through an example. If you are taking a photo of somebody, say your spouse, you might point your phone's camera at them, but realize that they are a silhouette against the background of the photo, and you cannot make out their face or other physical features. If you tap on the person, your phone's camera will re-focus and suddenly your subject will be illuminated, and you can see them now. This phenomenon is called *adjusting your exposure*. You don't need to know what that means, as long as you know how to do it. It could make or break a photo!

Another feature that you might like to know about when using your phone's camera, is how to turn the flash on or off. If you are trying to take a photo at night, you might need to use the flash. The teeny-tiny flash toggle can be found in the upper left corner of your screen. It looks like this:

Once you click this button, you can choose from turning the flash off, on, or putting it in auto-flash. Auto-flash will let the camera decide when the flash needs to be used. I would recommend putting it in auto-flash (if it isn't already).

Sometimes auto-flash doesn't work, and you might have to manually turn the flash on. You can click "on" if you need to do this.

SWITCHING CAMERAS

We will now talk about how to switch between the different back-facing cameras on your phone. There are three different methods of switching cameras, and it depends on the camera configuration that you have. We will break them up into three sections:

If you have one of these two camera configurations, then you can switch between the standard and telephoto cameras by taping this button:

It can be found right above the shutter button. Once you click this, you will switch to the telephoto camera. It will be evident that you switched cameras, because the camera screen will look like it zoomed in automatically. To return to the other camera, you can simply click the same button.

If you have this camera configuration, then you can switch between the
standard and the wide-angle cameras, by
tapping this button:

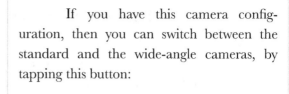

It can be found right above the
shutter button. Once you click this button,
you will switch to the wide-angle camera. It
will be evident that you switched cameras
because the camera screen will look like it
zoomed out automatically. To return to the
other camera, you can simply click the same
button.

Lastly, if you have this camera
configuration, then you can switch between
the standard camera, telephoto camera, and
wide-angle camera by tapping on different
parts of this toggle:

It can be found right about the
shutter button. If you want to use the wide-
angle camera, you can click the ".5" part of
this toggle. If you want to use the telephoto
(zoomed-in) camera, you can click the "2"
part of this toggle.

ZOOMING IN AND OUT

When you are taking a photo, you can also zoom in and out. This is helpful if you are trying to take a picture of something far away.

However, I caution you when you are zooming in. If it is possible to get closer to the thing you are trying to take a picture of, it would be best if you could go closer. This is because when you zoom in, you decrease the quality of the image that you take. For this reason, it is always best to walk as close as you can, and then zoom if you still need to get closer.

If you want to zoom in on a photo to see more detail, for example, you can place two fingers on your screen, and move your fingers farther apart from each other. To zoom back out, you can pinch your fingers back together (pinch your fingers together = zoom out, and move your fingers apart = zoom in).

VIDEO MODE

The buttons in the video mode are very similar to the buttons in the photo mode. The only main difference, is that the shutter button becomes red. If press the red record button, your phone will begin recording video, and the red circular button will turn into a square. When you stop recording video (by simply clicking the same button), the square button will turn back into a circle (just think: if I'm recording video, the shutter button will be a square, and if I'm not recording video, then it will be a circle).

Other than that, the video mode and photo mode are exactly the same. You can even focus and adjust your exposure the same way if you need to as well!

TIME-LAPSE/SLO-MO MODES

If you keep swiping left past the video mode, you might come across the time-lapse and slo-mode modes. Both of these modes are just different forms of recording video. Let me explain:

Time-lapse Mode: In Time-lapse mode, after you finish recording your video, the video will be sped up.

Slo-mo Mode: Slo-mo mode is the opposite of Time-laps mode; after you finish recording your video, the video will be slowed down.

Both of these modes are kinda cool to play around with, but is definitely not something you have to check out if you don't want to; they're just there if you want to play with them!

PORTRAIT MODE

The last mode that we will talk about is portrait mode. Portrait mode is a relatively new feature that was added to the camera app a couple of years ago. Portrait mode is only available on some phones.

Portrait mode is very similar to the regular photo mode. The only difference is that it blurs the background and separates your subject from the background.

Sometimes the blurred background makes the image a little bit nicer. Portrait mode is something fun that you can play around with!

> Note: One caveat of using portrait mode, is that you have to be about eight feet away from your subject. If you are too close your phone will give you a little alert towards the top of your screen. For example, it might tell you that you should "Move farther away". You can look for this alert and others that will pop up near the top of the camera screen. If there are no alerts at the top, then you are free to take the photo!

SCREENSHOTTING

The last thing that we will talk about in this chapter, is how to screenshot on your phone. Sometimes, you may want to screenshot what is on your phone so that you can show it to others. A screenshot is just like taking a picture of your phone's screen. Maybe you've come across something funny online. Maybe there is something on your phone that you are unaware of or confused about, and when you ask someone for help, they ask for a screenshot in return.

There are two different ways of screenshotting, and it depends if you have a home button on the bottom of your screen or not. If you have a home button, and wish to screenshot something, all you have to do is press the home button, and the power button at the same time.

If you have an iPhone that doesn't have a home button, then you have to press the volume up button, as well as the power button.

You will know if you've successfully screenshotted something, if you see your screen flash white, and you see the little icon of what the screenshot looks like in the bottom left corner:

The little screenshot icon in the bottom left corner will go away after a couple of seconds. The screenshot is saved to your Photos app, where you can view it and send it to someone if you'd like.

Yay! Congratulations! You know how to use your camera on your phone! Playing around with the camera on your phone is super fun to do. You can practice your skills by going outside and taking some pictures of flowers, trees, your home, etc. Have fun with it!

In the next chapter we will talk about the Photos app, which goes hand-in-hand with the Camera app!

CHAPTER SEVENTEEN

iPHONE PHOTOGRAPHY PART 2: THE PHOTOS APP

The photos app is an app that stores all of the photos that you have taken (or have saved from other sources) on your device. Let's jump right into it! This is what the app icon looks like:

When you open the app, you will be greeted with an interface that looks like this:

Just like the contacts app, there are various tabs within the Photos app that each have different functions. The tabs are Photos, For You, Albums, and Search. The tab that you are currently on should be blue, while the rest of the icons should be gray.

Personally, the only tab that I've ever used, is the Albums tab. I can't remember a time that I have used any of the other tabs.

CREATING, ORGANIZING, AND VIEWING ALBUMS

At the top of the Albums tab, you can see all of the albums that you have. On my phone, I only have two albums; Recents (all my photos), and Favorites (which contains the photos that I have favorited). Although I don't organize my photos into albums, I know that some people like too. The benefit of organizing your photos into albums, is that all the photos from one trip, for example, would be grouped together and easy to find. This is how my mom organizes the photos on her phone; and she has thousands of em!

If you would like to create an album, you can click the "+" button on the top left corner of the screen. Then you can click "New Album" (there is also an option for Shared Albums, but we will talk about what those are a little later). This will prompt you to enter in the name of the new album that you are creating. If you are creating an album from a vacation or a party that you went to, then you can name your album the name of the event, for example. Once you decide on an album title, you can click "Save".

The last step to creating an album, is to add the photos that you want to add. To chose the images you would like to add, you can simply tap on the photo.

If you don't have any photos on your phone yet, or haven't taken the images that you will eventually put into the album, then you can simply click the "Done" button on the top right corner of the screen. This will create your new album.

If you scroll down to the bottom of the Album tab, you will see these options:

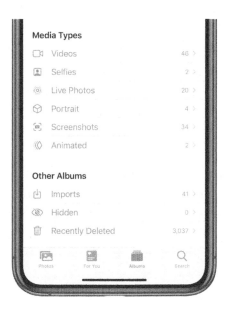

These options are pre-made albums that Apple has created for you. These albums group photos together that share certain characteristics, like Media Type. For example, if you click on the Videos album under Media Types, then you will be shown all the videos that you've taken on your phone. For another example, if you click Selfies, you will be shown all of the selfies that you've taken on your phone.

VIEWING ALL YOUR PHOTOS

Before we start, I should mention that there are many different ways to look at all of your photos. I am going to teach you the way that I view all of my photos, and the way that I think is the easiest to access.

To start, we will first make sure that we are on the Albums tab. To view all of the photos on your phone, click the "Recents" album at the top:

Once you click on your Recents album, you will be shown all of your images that you've ever taken (or saved) on your device. Your most recent pictures will be shown at the bottom, and your oldest images will be show at the top. This is what my Recents album looks like when I first open it:

If you want to view an image (in an enlarged view), you can simply click on it. This will enlarge the photo, and it will fill your screen:

There are a couple of different things that you can do here. If you look at the top of your screen, you can see the date and time at which you took the image. For the stack of pancakes above, you can see that I took the image on February 2nd, at 4:59 PM.

Just to the left of that, you can see the back arrow. If you click this, you will go back one screen, back to the Recents album (the grid of all of your photos).

If you look in the top right, you will see an "Edit" button. This is how you can edit your photo. We will talk about this in the next section.

EDITING YOUR PHOTOS

Sometimes, you may want to edit some of the basic features of your photo. Say, for example, you want to crop it a little bit.

If you would like to edit a photo, you can click the "Edit" button on the top right corner of your screen. This will bring up this interface:

This interface might look a little confusing, but we will walk through it together. At the bottom of your screen, there are three tabs shown in the editing interface. They look like this:

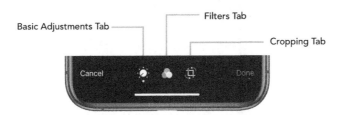

By default, you will be in the Basic Adjustments tab (the tab that is all the way on the left). Here, you can adjust things like exposure of your photo, the highlights the shadows, etc. These adjustments are rather tricky to understand and get the hang of, but they are pretty cool to play around with. Heres where you can find the basic adjustments of the Adjustment tab:

You can swipe left or right to navigate through the circular buttons to access other basic adjustment controls. We won't go into details about what each of these buttons do, because I don't use them that often, and I don't think that they are that useful for our needs (to be honest, I don't think I've ever used them).

The second (middle) tab, with the three overlapping circles, is the tab where you can add filters to your photos. I don't think I've ever used any of the filters here. You can just ignore this middle tab if you'd like.

The last tab, the one all the way on the right, is used to crop your photos. This is probably the most used tab for editing your photos. When you click the cropping tab, you should be met with an interface that looks like this:

To crop your photo, you can drag one of the corners inwards, or simply pinch your fingers in and out to resize it, to fit the image that you want to crop inside of the borders.

You can also rotate your images by 90-degree increments by tapping this button that can be found in the top left corner:

If you want to flip, or mirror your image, you can tap this button:

One last tool that you can use in the cropping tab, is to straighten or adjust the photo. You might see these circular buttons just below your photo:

These are the buttons that you can use to straighten or fix the horizontal/vertical perspective of the photo. Once you click them, you will have to use the slider (which can be found right below the three circular buttons) to adjust them incrementally. You can slide your finger left and right on the slider to see how the adjustments will affect your photo.

The Slider

Once you have finished using these tools and editing your photo to how you like it, you can tap the "Done" button in the bottom right corner to save your changes, or you can tap the "Cancel" button in the bottom left corner if you don't want to save the changes that you've made.

SHARING YOUR PHOTOS

If we look along the bottom of your screen when you are looking at an image in the enlarged view (look at the picture on page 174 if you forget what this view looks like), we can see a button that looks like this:

This button might look familiar to you. This is the button that you can use to share photos. Clicking this button will bring up the share card, where you can chose how you would like to share the photo.

This version of the share card works the same as it did in Safari. If you want to send this photo through text (which is probably the way that you are going to share photos the most), you can simply tap the Messages icon. If you wanted to email the photo to someone, you can also tap "Mail" (we will talk about setting up your email in the next chapter).

Let's go through an example together. Let's say that I wanted to send that image of the Golden Gate Bridge to my dad. So I tapped the share button, and now the share card has popped up. Because I want to simply text it to him, I can just tap the Messages icon.

After I do this, it will prompt me to enter in someone's name. I will type in "Dad" in the recipient's text box (at the top of the screen). Then, I will select the text box where the photo has been inserted into, and I can add a little message into here if I would like to. Maybe something like, "Missing this…" or something fun like that. Once I do that, I will click the send button. And my message is off! He will receive the photo on his phone now, and he can chose to save it then. We talked about saving photos on page 122 if you forget how to save photos from text messages!

FAVORITING PHOTOS

You may recall that I personally have two albums on my phone; the Recents album (where every single photo of yours is stored on your phone), and the favorites album. Although you can make your own favorites album if you would like (we talked about creating albums earlier in this chapter), Apple has an easy way of adding photos to your favorites album. If you are looking at a photo (in its enlarged view - page 174), you can see this button directly below the image:

If you click this, the photo will automatically be added to your favorites album. It is that easy! Want to remove it from your favorites album? You can just tap the heart icon again, and the photo will be removed from your favorites album.

SELECTING MULTIPLE PHOTOS AT ONCE

Sometimes, you might want to select multiple photos at once. You would want to do this if you are deleting a ton of images at once, or if you wanted to add a bunch of different photos to an album that you have previously made.

If this is the case, then there is a handy dandy way to do this. When you open your Recents album, and see the grid of all your photos, there is a "Select" button in the top right corner. If you click this, you will be able to select multiple different photos at once. In the image on the next page, I've selected three photos. You can tell if a photo is selected, by looking for the blue check mark in the bottom right corner of the image's thumbnail.

If I wanted to add the three selected photos to an album, I could click the share button (lower left corner). This would bring up the share card, and I can scroll down a little until I find the "Add to Album" button:

Note: There is a difference between the "Add to Shared Album" button and the "Add to Album" button. Shared Albums are albums that multiple people have access to, and where multiple people can add (or save) photos. I personally have only used them a couple of times, and it is definitely not the best way to share photos. My recommendation to share photos, is through text messages. However if you are curious, and want to create a shared album, you can click "New Shared Album" after you press the "+" button, and you will be brought through a couple of steps (like first naming the album, and then adding people whom you wish to share the album with).

DELETING PHOTOS

There are two ways to delete photos. The first methods is used if you want to delete a single photo. If you are looking at an image in the enlarged view, you may notice a trash-can symbol in the bottom right corner:

Once you click this button, the photo will be deleted.

The other method for deleting photos, is used if you want to delete a bunch of photos at once. If this is the case, you first have to select the photos you wish to delete. If you forget how to do this, look back to page 180. After you select multiple images, you can click the trash-can icon that is found in the bottom right corner.

WAIT! I DELETED A PHOTO I DIDN'T MEAN TO!

It is ok! Don't panic! There is a way to recover images that you delete for up to 30 days after you originally delete the photo.

To recover an image that you have accidentally deleted, you have to go to the "Recently Deleted" album.

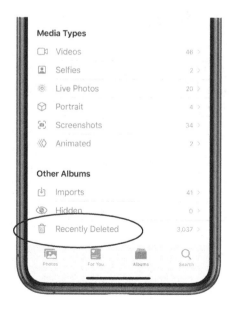

Once you open this album, you will see all of the photos that you've once deleted. You can select the ones that you wish to recover by tapping the "Select" button in the top right corner. Once you select the ones you wish to recover, you can tap the "Recover" button in the bottom right corner.

If you wish to delete the photo indefinitely, you can also select multiple photos, and delete them forever by tapping the delete button in the bottom left corner.

iPHONE PHOTOGRAPHY: WRAPPING IT ALL UP

Congratulations! These two chapters were definitely content-heavy. There is a lot to know about taking photos on your phone, and how to view or send them.

If you are feeling overwhelmed about all of the different options that there are, don't worry! It will take some time to familiarize yourself with everything and all of the buttons. I know it sure did for me!

The key to getting all of this down pat, is just experiencing and playing around with the camera and photos app. If you want more practice, you can take pictures of your home, some flowers, and some of the things your house. If you want practice sending them to people, you can send some of them too!

If you are still feeling overwhelmed, you can just use the app in the most basic form. You definitely want to know how to take a photo, and send it to someone. But if you don't care for the other features, don't worry about it! I am trying to give you the most amount of useful information possible, but if you won't use some of these options, then feel free to forget about 'em!

I hope that you are enjoying your phone and starting to get the hang of using it! In the beginning of this book, we covered most of the basic features that you will use on a daily basis. As we continue through this book, we will start to touch upon some of the other features that you might not use on a daily basis, but are still good to have or know about!

CHAPTER EIGHTEEN

EMAILS, AND HOW TO MANAGE 'EM ALL!

Emails are pretty important. In this chapter, we will discuss how to set your email up and how to manage the emails that you receive on your phone!

THE EMAIL SET UP PROCESS

You might already be receiving emails on your computer, but it is a hassle to have to take your computer out every time you want to check them. Let's set it up on your phone, so that you don't have to check your email on you computer. First let's open the app. This is what the Mail app looks like on your phone:

If you are opening it for the first time, you will have to go through the set-up process. When you open it, you will be greeted with this screen:

What you will have to do, is choose the company that you have an email account with. Through this set-up process, I will be setting up my email. I have a gmail account for my email, so I will select "Google". Once I do this, I will be greeted with a screen where I will have to log in with my email and password. You will use the same email that you have used before (maybe you have written down your email and password somewhere). This is what my login page looks like after I type my email in:

After I click "Next" to proceed to the next step, I will be prompted to enter in my password. Once I do this, this screen will pop up:

I would recommend to leave the settings how they are, and just click the "Save" button in the top right corner.

Once you do this, you will essentially be logged in and ready to start using your email!

MANAGING YOUR EMAILS

After you are all logged into your email, your inbox will look like this:

Your inbox shows all of your emails in one long list. At the top, I have an email from my mother regarding dinner reservations. If I tap on it, the email will open, and I can view the entire thing.

Another thing you might notice, are all the dots that are on the left of the emails. If there is a dot to the left of the email, it means that I haven't read it yet. In the picture above, I haven't read four of my emails. Once you tap into the email and read it, the blue dot on the left will disappear.

Do you see the "Mailboxes" button in the top left corner? Well, if you tap it, it brings you out to a menu where you can select the mailbox you would like to check:

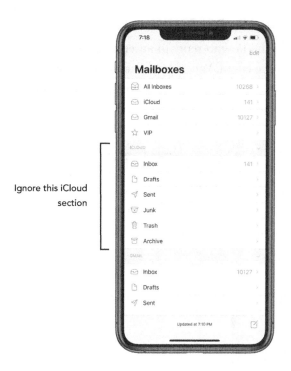

Ignore this iCloud section

Note: When you add your personal email to the Mail app, Apple might automatically add your iCloud email into the app as well. When you set up your phone for the first time in the set-up process, if you use your personal email to use for your Apple ID, then an iCloud email will not be added. The only time that an additional iCloud email is added into the Mail app, is if you add an email to the Mail app that is different than the email that you used to sign up for your Apple ID during the set-up process of your phone.

By looking at this screen, and scrolling down a little, you can get access to your junk mail, trash, sent emails, and archived emails. We all know that sometimes important emails can accidentally end up in with the rest of your junk mail!

If you want to get back to the screen that we were just on (the list of your emails), you can tap "All Inboxes"

FORWARDING, DELETING, AND REPLYING TO EMAILS

Knowing how to reply to an email is super important! First, you have to open the email. When you click on an email to read it, you might see this little arrow button in the bottom right corner of your screen:

When you click this button, you will be given these options:

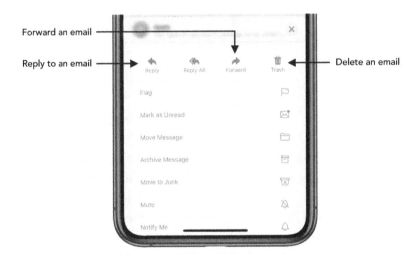

If you want to reply to an email, you can click the "Reply" button. Once you click this button, you can begin writing your email.

If you want to forward the email to someone else, you can press the "Forward" button. Then, you will be instructed to enter in the email of the person that you wish to forward the email to.

There are two main ways to delete emails. The first, is to click the "Trash" button on the screen that is shown in the picture above. This will delete the email.

The other way to delete an email, can be done in the inbox (the list of all the emails that you have received). If you are looking at your inbox, you can swipe left on the individual email, and three options will show up. Each one does a different thing:

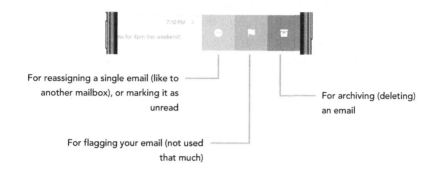

For reassigning a single email (like to another mailbox), or marking it as unread

For archiving (deleting) an email

For flagging your email (not used that much)

If you wish to delete the email, you can click on the archive button (the third one shown above).

When you click on this first button (), then you will be shown the same options that are shown on the previous page. From here, you can choose to reply to the email, forward it, delete it, mark it as unread, etc. If you mark an email as unread, then that means that the blue dot will reappear next to the email (we talked about the blue dot earlier, and how it represents an email that hasn't been read yet).

SELECTING/ARCHIVING MULTIPLE EMAILS AT ONCE

If you want to select multiple emails at once (say to delete a whole bunch of emails in one shot), you can hit the "Edit" button in the top right hand side of your screen (when you are looking at the list of emails in your inbox). Once you click "Edit", you will see selection bubbles on the left of every email. If you click on one of the emails, you will see that the selection bubble will become filled in. Once you select multiple emails, you can can chose between three options that appear at the bottom of your screen:

Mark   Move   Trash

If you would like to delete all of the emails that you've selected, you can click "Trash". If you would like to move them to another Mailbox, you can click "Move", and then select the mailbox you would like to send them to. Lastly, if you would just simply like to mark all of the selected emails as read (so that the blue bubble goes away), you can click "Mark", and then click "Mark as Read".

SORTING BY UNREAD EMAILS

There is a handy feature within the Mail app, that allows us to temporally view only the emails that we haven't read yet. This is what the toggle looks like:

It can be found in the bottom left corner of your screen (when you are looking at your inbox). If you press it, all of the emails you've already read will disappear. If you press it again, all of the emails that you have already read will come back. This is a toggle, meaning you can easily switch back and forth between the two settings.

DRAFTING A NEW EMAIL

If you would like to draft a new email, you can click this button:

It can be found in the bottom right corner of your screen (when you are looking at your inbox). This button also looks the exact same as the button you would click in Messages to create a new conversation. They both have the same function. Once you click this button, you will be greeted with a screen that looks like this:

This might look somewhat similar to what it looked like when you are creating a new conversation in Messages. First, you have to put the recipient's email in the box labeled "To:". Then you can fill in a subject, and then finally write the body of your email by clicking in the big white space just above your keyboard. Once you are done drafting your email, you can click the send button:

Then your email will send! If you didn't want to draft an email to begin with, or decide against sending it, you can click "Cancel" in the top left corner.

OPENING AND CLICKING ON LINKS IN AN EMAIL

Sometimes your email might have a link inside of it that will open a webpage. If this is the case, and you click on the link, then the webpage will open inside of the Safari app. Therefore, you will no longer be in the Mail app, and you will now be in the Safari app. Here you can browse the webpage and look around. Once you are done and would like to return back to the Mail app, you can take advantage of the feature called 'breadcrumbs'. I know, it sounds quite silly. Breadcrumbs is a feature that allows you to switch between different apps on your phone.

For example, if you were just in the Mail app, and if you clicked on a link, you would be brought to the webpage in the Safari app. If you would like to go back into the Mail app, you can use the breadcrumbs button. This is what it looks like, and where it can be found:

Now, the button won't say "Mail" every time; it will say the first app's name that you were just in, before you clicked on a link (or button or something else) to open a second app. This way, while you are in the second app, you can click on the first app's name to go back to it.

CHAPTER NINETEEN

HOW'S THE WEATHER UP THERE?

In this chapter, we will talk about the Weather app. Your iPhone has this super cool ability to be able to tell you the weather of practically anywhere on Earth. Its pretty cool. In this chapter we will talk about how it works, and how to set it up so that it gives you the weather in your area!

This is what the weather app looks like:

When you first open the app, you will first be greeted with this alert:

Make sure that you click "Allow While Using App". This is super duper important. If you allow the Weather app to use your location, then you will be able to get the weather based on your location.

After you tap "Allow While Using App", you will be greeted with the weather in Cupertino, California (this is where Apple's headquarters are). Because we allowed for the Weather app to use our location, if we swipe left, we can see the weather for your current location.

As you can see, it is a nice day outside today :)

If you look at the top, below the temperature, you can see the hour-by-hour forecast. You can use your finger to scroll left and right on this hour-by-hour forecast to see additional hours that you can't immediately see.

If you scroll down, you can see more specific pieces of information, like chance of precipitation, humidity, visibility, etc.

Thats pretty much it! The weather app is pretty simple, but it's a nice way to look at the weather ahead of time without having to watch the news or check it online ahead of time!

CHAPTER TWENTY

TAKIN' NOTES

Has someone ever told you to write something down real quick? Or maybe you had a quick thought and want to write it down for later? Well, now there is a much easier way to take quick notes like these instead of rummaging through a drawer to find a piece of paper and a pen.

In this chapter, we will talk about the Notes app. For me, the Notes app is such a life saver, and I use it all the time. I even see my dad using the Notes app, for keeping track of things like grocery lists or food takeout orders! It is definitely something that you should take advantage of!

Let's take a dive through the Notes app. This is what the app icon looks like:

When you open the app, you will be greeted with a screen that looks like this:

Because I've had my phone for a while now, you can see that I already have some notes in there.

CREATING A NEW NOTE

Let's start with learning how to create a new note. Do you see this button in the bottom right corner? If you click this, it will create a new note for you.

Once you click this, a new screen will pop up:

This is your new note. You can start typing right away!

> Note: The Notes app automatically bolds the first line of text that you enter in. Therefore, I would suggest putting the title of your note on this first line, before you start typing the body of your note.

When you are done typing your note, you can click the "Done" button in the top right corner.

MAKING A CHECKLIST WITH INTERACTIVE CHECK BUTTONS

If you are making a checklist, or maybe a grocery list, you may want to be able to check items off, or cross them out. Luckily for you, there is an easy way of doing this!

Above the keyboard, there is a button that looks like this:

If you click on it, a circular button will appear, and you can write a piece of text to the right of it.

If you tap "return" on the keyboard (after you write a piece of text next to the first bubble), your cursor will jump down a line (just like when typing on a computer). Then, a new bubble will appear. When you've finished entering in all the items you want to enter in, you can tap "Done".

Then, when you are at the grocery store, you can tap in the empty circle to fill in the bubble, and to ultimately check the item off. It will look something like this:

It's a pretty neat feature, and makes grocery lists interactive and easy to manage!

DELETING A NOTE

Once you are done with a note, you might want to delete it. There are three different ways to delete a note.

The first way to delete a note, is used if you only want to delete a single note. To do this, you can open the note that you wish to delete, and tap the trash-can icon in the bottom left corner of your screen (look at the picture above). This will delete the note.

The second way to delete a note is by swiping on the note itself when you are looking at the list view of all your notes. If you swipe to the right on a note in the list view, these options will show up:

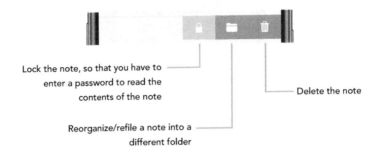

Lock the note, so that you have to
enter a password to read the
contents of the note

Delete the note

Reorganize/refile a note into a
different folder

If you want to delete the note, then you can tap the trash can icon here.

If you would like to delete multiple notes at once, you will use the third method. First, you must go to the list-view (look at the picture on page 204). In the top right hand corner, you may notice three dots:

If you tap this button, you will be shown two options. Click "Select Notes...":

Once you are done selecting the notes that you want to delete, you can tap "Delete" in the bottom right corner, and your selected notes will be deleted!

SORTING NOTES INTO FOLDERS

There is a feature in the Notes app that allows you to file different notes into different folders. This is almost like how in Middle School, kids can have different folders for each class. Being able to categorize notes into different folders allows you to group similar notes into one place.

However, I don't think this feature is that useful, unless you are taking pages and pages of notes into the Notes app (which you're probably not).

If you would like to explore this feature and see if it is right for you, though, you can tap the "Folders" button in the top left corner of your screen. This will open a side menu that has all of the folders that your phone has in the Notes app (you probably only have two or three of the folders that Apple generated for you). If you want to create a new folder, you can simply tap "New Folder" in the bottom right corner.

Again, I don't think categorizing your notes into folders is ideal. I once tried to file my notes into different folders, but it became a chore to keep sorting them and took too long to find a specific note that I was looking for.

CHAPTER TWENTY ONE

NO MORE GETTING LOST ON THE ROAD, I PROMISE YOU!

In this chapter, we will talk about the Maps app (this app allows you to use GPS for navigation). If you already have a GPS and you enjoy using that for navigation, then you are more than welcome to continue using that. But I promise you, the features inside of the Maps app are insane, and actually really cool. I think it's amazing how detailed the Maps app is, and how easy it is to drive using the Maps app as your GPS.

One of the reasons I waited this long to talk about the Maps app, is because I wanted you to be comfortable with using your phone for simpler tasks. There is no denying it, using the Maps app is pretty difficult. But I think navigating using any GPS is difficult. But don't worry. I will break everything down for you just like we have in the first half of this book, and we will be driving around in no time!

Let's get started! This is what the Maps app looks like:

When you open the maps app for the first time, you will be met with this alert:

It is important that you choose "Allow While Using App", so that you will be able to navigate to places using your location.

Once you click "Allow While Using App", you will then be shown your location, just like this:

NAVIGATING TO SOMEWHERE

The first thing that we will learn, is how to go from point A to point B. Most often, your 'point A' will be your location (where you are right now). This is why we allowed the app to access our location. However, we have to manually enter in 'point B'.

Something that you might have had to do on an old physical GPS, is plug in the exact address of the place that you want to go to (you know, the number, street name, etc). For example, if you were going to someones house, then you would just type in that person's address into the search bar, and then bam; you're on your way. It is just as easy to do this on your phone, as it is on the physical GPS.

However, something cool about the Maps app on your phone, is that sometimes you don't have to enter in the exact address of the location you want to travel to.

For example, let's say I wanted to take a trip to the closest Walmart. What I can do, is type in "Walmart" into the search bar (the search bar is found at the bottom of your screen), and it will show me all of the Walmarts that are close to my current location:

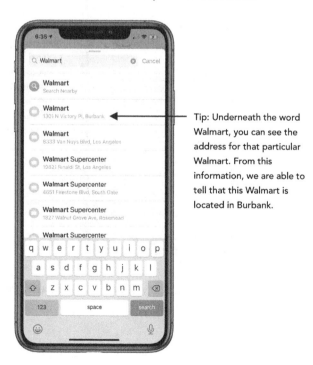

Tip: Underneath the word Walmart, you can see the address for that particular Walmart. From this information, we are able to tell that this Walmart is located in Burbank.

If you already know the Walmart that you want to go to, or just want to go to the one that is closest one to you, then you can just click on one of the Walmarts that pop up in the search results right after you search for them (look at the picture on the previous page). Personally, I want to go to the closest Walmart to me (for times sake), so I will click on the Walmart that is in Burbank, or the second search result that pops up after I search for "Walmart".

If I didn't know which Walmart I wanted to go to, and wanted to look at all of the Walmarts around me on the map (to compare their location to mine), then I can click the first search result, titled "Walmart, Search Nearby" (with the little magnifying-glass icon next to it). This screen will pop up, and I can tap and choose which Walmart I would like to navigate to by looking at all of them visually:

Helpful Tip: You can use two fingers to zoom in and out to look around the map. If you zoom in, you will be able to see a more detailed map of the place that you are traveling to.

Once I choose the Walmart I want to go to, I can simply tap on it, and this screen will pop up:

Once I am here, I can learn a little bit more information about the location that I am traveling to. If I swipe up on the bottom section of my screen (where it has the pictures and the big blue "Directions" button, I can view additional information like the stores' hours, phone number, and even the exact address.

After looking at the additional information, I've decided that this is the Walmart that I want to go to. The next thing that I will do to get directions, and ultimately follow the GPS to this Walmart, is to click the blue "Directions" button. Once I do this, this screen will pop up:

Here you can see an estimate of how long it will take to get to your destination. Now, I can press the green "GO" button, and the navigation will begin. It will look like this:

Here, at the bottom portion of your screen, you can see things like your estimated time of arrival, the number of minutes you have left in your trip, and the distance you have left to travel until you reach your destination.

Now my phone will navigate me through the roads until I get to my destination; the Walmart.

> Note: If you are navigating to someones house, for example, and you know the houses's exact address, you can simply type the address into the search bar when you first open the Maps app. Once you do this, you can select their address from the search results, and then click the green "GO" button to begin navigating to your location!

ADDITIONAL CONTROLS WHILE NAVIGATING

When you are in the middle of a trip (using navigation), you can swipe upwards on the lower portion of the screen (where it says your arrival time and the distance until your destination) to reveal additional controls and functions:

Say you want to view a list of the directions, instead of the turn-by-turn navigation view. You can tap the "Details" button, and the list of directions will pop up. When you are done looking at the list of directions, you can tap the "Done" button in the top right corner, and it will return you back to the turn-by-turn navigation view.

Another useful button in this additional control panel, is the "Gas Stations" button. If you are running low on gas, or want to stop for gas along your route, you can tap this button. When you tap it, you can select a gas station based on its proximity to you. This will allow you to make a quick stop along your trip, without having to exit out of current navigation session that you are in! This means that your navigation session will take a quick pitstop at the gas station, and once the pitstop is over, you will be able to resume the rest of your trip; just like nothing ever happened!

HOW TO END YOUR NAVIGATION SESSION

When you are done with your trip, you can hit the "End" button that can be found in the bottom right corner of your screen. It looks like this:

"PINNING" LOCATIONS

If you are looking around the map, and see something interesting, you can "drop a pin" on it. To do this, all you have to do is press and hold on the location that you wish to drop the pin onto. Here is an example of a pin that I dropped onto the Grand Canyon, in the United States:

As you can see, it saves the location, and you can see a little pin icon on the map. If you wanted to get directions to this spot, you can also click the "Directions" button, and the navigation (to where you dropped the pin) will begin.

If you want to delete the pin that you just dropped, you can click the trash-can icon in the bottom left corner of your screen.

If you want to share this location with someone else, you can tap the share icon in the bottom right corner of your phone, and the share card (which you have seen so many times now) will pop up! You know what to do from there! :)

We will talk about what that middle button ("Add to…") does in a little bit!

YOUR FAVORITE/MOST USED LOCATIONS

There is this cool feature on your phone that allows you to quickly navigate to some of your favorite places, or just places that you travel to often. It is super simple to set up, and can save you a lot of time. To find the list of your favorite locations, simply swipe up from the search bar when you first open the app (when you are not in a navigation session). After you swipe up, you should see something like this:

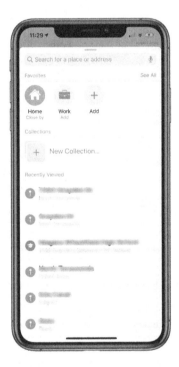

The Favorites section is at the top of the screen. You can see that I've added my house's location to the "Home" button, so that I can quickly navigate back home after driving somewhere. If you would like to add a location to this favorites bar, you can simply click the "Add" button that has a "+" symbol in the middle of it.

After you click this button, you will be prompted to enter in an address, or general search term (like "Walmart", where you can then look around for the specific Walmart that you wish to save; this is easier and quicker than trying to find the exact address of the Walmart that you wish to add). Once you've finished looking for and finding the place you want to add, you can click the "Done" button in the top right corner, and then click "Done" (again) on the next page.

PLANNING A VACATION OR ROAD TRIP? MAKE A COLLECTION OF LOCATIONS

Making a collection of locations is super simple. If you swipe up on the search bar (just like we did for adding to our favorite locations), you will see a "Collections" section.

To create a new collection, simply click "New Collection"

You will then be prompted to put in a title for the collection. If you are planning a road trip, you can type in "Road Trip" or something like that. Then you can hit "Create" in the top right corner. This will create your collection.

Now we will talk about how to add locations into the collection that you have just made. If we go back to the Grand Canyon example a couple of pages ago, you may remember there is one button that we didn't talk about; the "Add to…" button.

If you click the "Add to…" button, you will then be able to choose the collection that you wish to add the marked location to. Pretty cool right? Its all starting to come full circle!

Sometimes, you might want to add a location to a collection that you haven't dropped a pin at. Let's continue with the Walmart example. If you want to add Walmart to your list of locations for your road trip (it sounds pretty silly, but we will roll with it), you first have to select the Walmart that you wish to add. I've found a Walmart in Arizona that I would like to add to my collection. This is what the screen looks like once I've pulled up the screen that gives me information about the Walmart (turn back to page 216/217 to learn more about how to access this screen if you forget!):

Cool. Now, to add it to my collections, I can swipe up on that bottom section of my screen (where it has the pictures, and the "Directions" button), and then we will see the famous "Add to" button. Once I click that, I can select "Road Trip" as the collection that I would like to add this location to:

YOUR RECENTLY VIEWED LOCATIONS

The last thing that we can see from swiping up from the search bar, is your recently viewed locations.

This is a quick and easy way to navigate to a place that you have looked at previously.

It is a small feature, but might prove useful at some point!

SEARCHING FOR FOOD (OR SOMETHING ELSE)

Let's say that you are in a new country. You've just flown half way across the world, and don't really know a lot of information about your surroundings, like restaurants and stuff (besides some quick google searches you did leading up to the trip). Now, its time for dinner, and you're looking for a restaurant to eat at. It has happened to me and my family so many times.

If you find yourself in this predicament, there are two ways that you can go about it. My mom's method, is to pull out her phone and type into Safari, "Best places to eat in ____". This proves to be pretty useful, and usually generates a few good restaurants.

My dad's method is to type "Food" into the Apple Map's search bar. With this method, you will find restaurants around your location (and be able to see how far away you are from them). By doing it this way, you are able to see some reviews, some pictures, their hours, and other small pieces of information about the restaurant. Typically, you will be able to find their website (with their menu) using this method too.

This is what the icons of the restaurants look like.

To view a restaurant and its information, you can click on the restaurant's icon. You can see what the icon's look like to the right.

The best way to practice using the Maps app, is to just play around with it. I recommend looking at the various restaurants around you, and pretend to navigate to them to learn how the Maps app works. You might also find some restaurants that are around you that you haven't heard about! Again, practice makes perfect!

CHAPTER TWENTY TWO

DIGITALIZE YOUR CALENDAR; YOU'LL NEVER GO BACK!

Digitalizing my calendar onto my phone has been huge for me.

Now that you finally have an iPhone, it is time to ditch that paper calendar of yours, and make it completely digital! You won't go back, I can promise you that!

This is what the Calendar App looks like:

Thursday
14

When you first open the app, you will be greeted with a screen that looks like this:

This is the daily-view. Inside of the calendar app, there are three different views; the daily view, the monthly view, and the yearly view. This is what each of them look like:

Daily view   Monthly view   Yearly view

If you are in the daily view, you can go to the monthly view by tapping the current month in the top left corner. Then once you are in the monthly view, you can go to the yearly view by tapping on the current year in the top left corner.

If you are in the yearly view, you can tap into the monthly view, by tapping on any one of the months that you would like to have a closer look at. Once you are in the monthly view, you can tap on a specific day (the number of the day) to enter the daily view (and look closer at that specific day).

> Note: You can also tap the "Today" button in the bottom left corner to return to the daily-view for today.

Personally, I don't really use the yearly or daily views; I use the monthly view the most.

VIEWING CALENDAR EVENTS THAT YOU HAVE ENTERED IN

To view the calendar events that you have entered in, we can tap this button that can be found along the top of the screen:

Once you tap this, you will see the bottom of your screen change, and you will be able to see the events that you have listed (I didn't have any events entered into my calendar today, but they would show up here if I did).

To switch between the different months of the year, you can swipe up and down on the monthly calendar portion of your screen (where the dates of the days are). You can always tell which month you are in, by looking at the name in the top left corner. The month written on this button will always update to the month that you are looking at in the monthly view (in the example above, I was looking at May 2020. If I was looking at March 2020, it was say "March 2020" in the top left corner).

To see the events that you have for the day, I would first recommend that you are in the monthly view. Next, you can simply tap on the date that you would like to see the events for. For example, If I want to check if I have any events on May 27th, I can simply tap in the "27" on the calendar.

Note: Do you see the little dots below some of the dates when you are looking at the monthly view? This means that there are events scheduled for that day. If you do not see a dot below a specific number, then there are no events scheduled for the specific day. In the example I mentioned a second ago, we already know that there are no events on May 27th, because there is not a dot below the number.

CREATING A NEW CALENDAR EVENT

To create a new calendar event, you can press the "+" button in the top right corner. Once you tap it, the "New Event" screen will pop up. It looks like this:

This is where you can add the information that you want to add to the specific event, like the title, the time that it starts, etc.

Another cool feature of the digital Calendar app, is the ability to repeat the same event multiple times. If you click the "Repeat" button on this screen, you will be given a few options:

Here you can choose how frequent you want the event to repeat. This is useful if you have the same event multiple times a month. Once you are done selecting how frequent you want the event to repeat, you can go back by hitting the "New Event" button in the top right corner.

> Note: You might be starting to notice a trend when you want to navigate back a page. If you want to go back a single page, there is usually a button in the top left corner of your screen with a "<" before whatever the previous page's name is.

The last interesting feature about creating a new event, is the ability for your phone to alert (or notify, in 'phone terms') you about the event before the event happens. If you scroll down a little when you are entering in the information for the event, you will see the "Alert" button. Once you click this, these options will show up:

You can select between these options of how you would like your phone to alert you of the event. I like this feature a lot! Once you are done here, you can go back (by hitting "< New Event" in the top left corner).

Once you are done entering in all of the information for the event, you can tap the "Add" button in the top right corner to save and add the event to your calendar. You will now see your new event show up in the bottom portion of your screen. It should look like this:

EDITING AND DELETING AN EVENT

It is very easy to edit and delete an event. First, make sure you are in the monthly view, and looking at the list of events that you have on that specific day (see the picture above for reference). Then, tap on the event. Now you will be able to see more details about the event that you just clicked on:

  If you want to edit the event, you can tap the "Edit" button in the top right corner of your screen. This will bring up a similar page to what it looked like when you were first creating the event.

  If you want to delete the event, you can simply tap "Delete Event" at the very bottom of your screen.

CHAPTER TWENTY THREE

SETTING ALARMS!

Setting alarms... hmm... If you're like me and you're a night person (Im currently writing this at 3 am), then alarms are probably not your thing. My alarm is set for 10 am tomorrow morning (its the weekend right now, otherwise it is typically set for 6:30 am).

If you are a morning person who typically gets up early, then alarms might not be that big of a deal to you.

But for me, there is just about nothing that can wake me up in the mornings. I've tried everything. But, the thing that has worked the best, is the phone alarm, set to max volume. It sounds kind of crazy, but the blaring fire alarm noise that I have it set is starting to nag at me, and it works; I am finally waking up to my alarms! Wohoo!

Why am I telling you this? Well, its a little off topic, and I apologize. But, in this chapter we will talk about how to set alarms, and we will play with things like timers and stop watches. All of these fun toys (okay, the alarm isn't necessarily fun), can be found in the Clock app. This is what the Clock app looks like:

Once you open it, you will be greeted with this screen:

This is known as the "World Clock" Tab. Here you can look at what time it is in different time zones. If you would like to add a location to this list, you can simply click the "+" button in the top right corner.

> Note: If you are adding a time zone to this list, you have to search for a major city near you; if you don't live in a large city, then the specific town that you live in might not be listed.

THE CLOCK APP'S TABS

If you look at the bottom of your screen, you can see that there are five different tabs in this app. These tabs are World Clock, Alarm, Bedtime, Stopwatch, and Timer. We've already talked about World Clock, but we will talk about the other tabs next.

THE STOPWATCH TAB

The stopwatch tab is the simplest tab in this app. If you tap on the stopwatch icon to switch tabs (the icon will change to orange when it is selected), then this screen will pop up:

The buttons here are rather self explanatory; if you tap start, the stopwatch will start, and if you tap lap, the stopwatch will add a lap to the list that will be created below the stopwatch's numbers.

There are two different ways that you can view the stopwatch. The digital stopwatch version (which is shown in the picture above), and an analog version. You can switch to the analog version of the stopwatch, by swiping left on the digital stopwatch. If you want to change back to the digital version, you can swipe right.

THE TIMER TAB

The timer tab is also useful. When you click on this tab, this screen will show up:

There are a couple different options that you have here. You can set the duration of the timer by sliding up and down on the wheels (where the numbers are). You can also change the sound that the timer makes when the timer is up. You can tap the "When Timer Ends" button to change the timer sound. When you are looking at the list of sounds, you can click on any one of them to hear what they would sound like. Once you are satisfied with a sound (there should be a checkmark next to the sound that you choose), you can select "Set" in the top right corner.

Once you are all set to begin your timer, you can hit the green "Start" button. This will begin your timer.

THE BEDTIME TAB

The bedtime tab probably won't be useful to you. This tab allows you to set what time you wish to wake up, and Apple will alert your phone when you should start winding down for bed. I personally don't use this feature, but if you would like to play around with the options that it gives you, you can feel free to do so.

THE ALARM TAB

Ahh yes. We have made it to the final tab; the Alarm tab. This is probably the most-used tab inside of the Clock app. When you first click on this tab, this screen will show up:

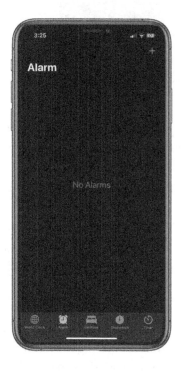

We have to create our first alarm. To do this, you can click the "+" button in the top right corner. Once you do this, your interface will change, to the "Add Alarm" interface. This is what it looks like:

If you have iOS 14 installed on your phone, then you won't see the scrolling number wheels, but rather a keypad where you can just type in the numbers that you wish to input.

The first thing that you should do, is change the time that the alarm is set for. To do this, you can slide your finger on the wheel (with the numbers on it).

Next, you can move on to the other four settings that you can change.

The "Repeat" setting is if you want to repeat the alarm on certain days. I do this for my school alarms, so that I don't have to turn them on every night before I go to bed (they will just automatically turn on for me).

The "Label" setting is if you want to change the name of the alarm. For example, you might want to change it to "Walk the dog", or "Take the meat out of the oven"; things like that.

The "Sound" setting is used to change the alarm sound that will go off at the time you set for your alarm to go off. You can leave it at the default sound if you'd like; trust me, its annoying enough to get you up!

Lastly, the "Snooze" button can be toggled on or off (depending on if you want the snooze option available to you when the alarm goes of). I would recommend just keeping this on.

Once you are done changing some of the settings, you can hit the "Save" button in the top right corner of your screen. This will save your alarm, and turn it on for the time that you set it at.

Now that we have our alarm saved, it should show up on our screen now:

Cool! You can see that the 10:00 am alarm is set to the on position by the little indicator switch to the right of it. This means that it will go off at 10:00 am. However, the alarm for 11:15 am underneath it is off. This means that it will not go off at 11:15 am. If I wanted this alarm to go off too, then I could toggle that on, by just tapping the switch icon.

SHUTTING OFF ALARMS WHEN THEY GO OFF

When alarms go off at the time that you set them for, you will be shown this interface on your lockscreen:

If you want to stop the alarm, you can press the "Stop" button on the bottom of your screen.

However, if you want to snooze it (so that it'll go off 9 minutes later), then you can hit the "Snooze" button. If you hit snooze, there will be a clock notification on your lock screen that will tell you how much time is left on your snoozed-alarm before it will go off again. This is what the notification looks like:

Once the snooze time is up, your alarm will go off again, and you will be given the options to Snooze the alarm again, or Stop it.

MAKING ALARMS LOUDER!

If you think that your alarm isn't loud enough, or you want to make it louder, there is a way to do this in the Settings app. We will talk more about the Settings app, and how to specifically make your alarm louder, in a later chapter!

CHAPTER TWENTY FOUR

LISTENING TO MUSIC

Listening to music is pretty fun and can be pretty relaxing. I like to put music on when I'm doing other things, like homework or cleaning up my room. There is an easy way to do this, in the Music app.

Now, there are two different ways of listening to music. You can either buy every song that you want to listen to (it is about $1.29 per song), or you can use a music streaming service (like Apple's Apple Music). Both of these are viable options, and you should try and think about which option you want to use.

UNDERSTANDING THE MUSIC APP'S TABS

Just like a lot of the other apps made by Apple, the Music app has five different tabs that can be found along the bottom of the screen. This is what they look like:

THE LIBRARY TAB

The Library tab is where all of the downloaded music on your device lives. Wether you downloaded them from the streaming service Apple Music, or bought them individually, they can all be found here.

THE FOR YOU TAB

This tab will only be useful to you, if you subscribe to Apple Music, Apple's music streaming service. If you do not subscribe to this, then this tab doesn't hold a purpose for you!

However, if you do purchase the streaming service, then you can see recommendations for songs that are based on the music that you've been listening too (the app will keep track of what type of music you've been listening to, and will give you suggestions of other songs to listen too that are similar).

You can also view some of the recent music that you've been listening to on this page as well.

THE BROWSE TAB

This tab will also only be useful to you, if you subscribe to Apple Music, the music streaming service. If you do not subscribe to this, then this tab doesn't hold a purpose for you!

However, if you do purchase the streaming service, then this tab will allow you to browse some of the most popular music that is out right now. You can also use this page to download some new music (if you have the streaming service).

THE RADIO TAB

This tab will be useful to both people; those that have bought the streaming service, and those who haven't!

This tab is kind of like the radio in your car. Here, you can choose different radio stations that you want to listen to, completely free! When you tap onto this page, you will see a screen that looks like this:

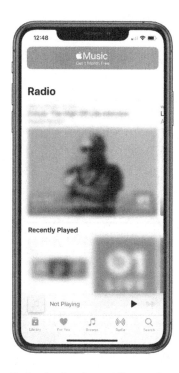

You can scroll both horizontally and vertically through the interface to view different radio stations or scheduled interviews.

Something in this tab that you should definitely check out, is the "Broadcast Radio" section. Anything listed in this section will be similar to things that you can hear on the radio (meaning that they play 24/7). Under this section in the Radio tab, you can listen to stations like NPR, ESPN Radio, and so many other music-related music stations. You can play with them and experiment until you find ones that you like!

If you scroll all the way towards the bottom of the Radio tab, you can see a section called "Apple Music Radio". This is the only section in the Radio tab that you have to pay for. In order to listen to these radio stations, you must pay the subscription to Apple Music, the streaming service.

THE SEARCH TAB

The last tab, is the Search tab. Here, you can search for songs that you might want to listen to.

You can easily toggle between searching for songs in your library (songs that you've already downloaded to your phone), or the Apple Music library (if you have an Apple Music streaming service subscription).

In other words, if you do not have a streaming service subscription, then you can only search for songs that are in "Your Library". You may be thinking, "Then how do I buy songs?," and you are totally right. We will talk about how to buy songs a little bit later.

If you do pay monthly for Apple Music, then you can search for any song you'd like by switching the giant toggle just underneath the search bar to "Apple Music". Then when the search results come up, you will be able to play any song that you would like to! It's that easy! If you find a song here that you would like to add to your own library, you can tap the "+" icon (that can be found next to any song), and it will show up in the Library tab for easy access!

STREAMING MUSIC: APPLE MUSIC

Music streaming is where you pay a monthly price to get access to every song that has ever been released! Apple has their own music streaming service called Apple Music, where you can pay a premium to get access to their entire music library (40,000,000+ songs). It is insane! As of the time of me writing this book, Apple Music (the streaming service) is $9.99 a month. If you are not interested in paying monthly, then you can buy each individual song that you would like to listen to. We will talk about buying songs individually in the next section.

In this section, we will talk about how to sign up for Apple Music if you would like to.

To sign up for Apple Music, you first have to go to the For You tab.

Once you are here, you can tap the "Choose Your Plan" button, and you will then be shown three options of possible payment methods for Apple Music:

Most likely, you will just choose the Individual plan. When you are ready, you can tap the "Join Apple Music" button at the bottom of the screen. This will prompt you do either pay the bill with Face ID or Touch ID:

Because I have a phone with Face ID, I will simply use that to pay the bill.

If you have Touch ID, then you can use your thumb's fingerprint to pay for it, by placing your finger on the finger print sensor (the circular home button).

> Note: The Apple Music streaming service will charge your credit/debit card automatically. Make sure that you remember your card is being charged every month. In other words, Apple will not ask if you want to continue paying every month, it will just deduct the money from your bank account.

If you don't have a credit or debit card set up in your phone, then you will not be able to pay for Apple Music. If you are interested in plugging in a credit or debit card up on your phone, don't worry; we will talk about setting that up in a couple of chapters.

BUYING EACH SONG INDIVIDUALLY

The next thing that I am going to talk about, is buying songs individually. If we want to buy songs individually, then we have to use the music store, which is also known as the iTunes Store. This is what the iTunes Store looks like:

When you open this app, you will be met with a bunch of different pictures, words, etc; it is a very busy screen.

If you look at the bottom, we can see the very familiar five-tab-setup:

Let's quickly go through what each of these tabs do.

The "Music" tab is where you can explore new Music. You can look at music that was just released, or the music top charts.

The next two tabs, "Movies" and "TV Shows", are used to download and watch movies and TV shows. We will talk about these tabs in the next chapter.

The fourth tab, is the "Search" tab. Here, you can search for songs that you might want to listen to (you can also search for movies and TV shows here, but again, we will talk about movies and TV shows in the next chapter). When you click on the search tab icon, you will see a search bar pop up at the top of your screen. Here you can type in the name of the song you want to purchase. Once you do this and hit the blue search button, search results will start to pop up. When you search for something using the search tab, you will get results for ringtones, songs, albums, podcasts, TV shows, Movies, etc. You can scroll vertically to switch between the different categories (there will be gray lines separating each category of content). Once you find either the song, movie, or tv show that you wish to buy, you can tap it to get more information about it.

The last tab, is called "More", and here you can buy ringtones (for your your alarm sounds or text message alert sounds), and other things. There isn't really anything fancy on this tab, and you can pretty much ignore it if you'd like.

When you find a song that you would like to download, either by searching for it on the Search tab, or by browsing through the top charts on the Music tab, you may find the purchase button. This is what it looks like:

$1.29

Once you click this button, the song will start to download. Once it is done, you can go back into the Music app, switch to the "Library" tab (the bottom left corner), and you should see the song that you just bought will be downloaded there. You can tap on the song to play it.

Note: The pricing of the song is shown inside of the download button. In the example above, the song was $1.29, however it isn't always $1.29. Just keep this in mind when you are browsing for songs!

WRAPPING UP THE CHAPTER...

Regardless of what music-listening option you use, music is so fun and you should definitely experiment with one of these methods.

If you aren't interested in spending any money, then definitely play with the Radio stations that can be found within the Music apps' Radio tab. Most of the radio stations are 100% free, and can be a good source of background music!

We talked a little bit about it already, but in the next chapter we will talk about how to download movies and tv shows, and how you would go about watching them!

CHAPTER TWENTY FIVE

GET SOME POPCORN, AND WATCH A MOVIE!

Say you are planning a vacation. You deserve it! But, there is a long flight ahead of you. And here comes the worst part: there aren't any TVs on this plane! That means you can't watch anything, right?

No! You are wrong, because you have your phone! There is an easy and simple way to download movies and TV shows straight to your phone (unfortunately, it isn't free, like it usually is on planes though).

LOOKING FOR A MOVIE OR TV SHOW TO BUY

We talked a little bit about this in the last chapter. If you are looking to buy a movie or TV show to watch on your phone, then we first have to open the iTunes app. If you remember from the last chapter, we talked a little bit about how there are two tabs, called "Movies", and "TV Shows", that you can use to browse through the most popular movies and TV shows.

You can also use the same search bar in the iTunes app to search for a certain TV show or Movie that you would like to purchase. When you search for something using the search tab, you will get results for ringtones, songs, albums, podcasts, TV shows, Movies, etc. You can scroll vertically to switch between the different categories (there will be gray lines separating each block of content). Once you find either the song, movie, or TV show that you wish to buy, you can tap on it to get more information.

WATCHING TRAILERS AND MORE MOVIE INFORMATION

When you are looking for a movie, the experience is a little different than looking for a song or TV show. When you find a movie that you would like to learn more about, you have to tap on the movie cover, and a screen that looks like this will pop up on your phone

Here, you can see additional pieces of information, like details about the movie, reviews, trailers, and even other movies that are similar to this one (by tapping the "Related" button).

If you want to watch the trailer for the movie, you can click the picture (with the play button on it) underneath the word "Trailers". This will open the video on your screen, and you will be able to watch the trailer.

You may also notice that there are two buttons to download the movie; rent and buy. If you buy the movie, the you will own it forever; you can watch it how ever many times you want! The rent button will give you 30 days to start watching the movie, and once you start it, you will have 48 hours to finish it. Once this time is up, you will no longer be able to watch the movie.

Typically, I will just rent the movie. However, sometimes, if I really like the movie or think I will watch it a bunch, I will buy it. These two options are just something to keep in mind when you are deciding how to download your movie.

Of course, the rent/buy option is only for movies; for TV shows, your only option is to buy it.

WATCHING YOUR MOVIES OR TV SHOWS

Now that your movie or TV show is downloaded, you may be asking yourself, "How do I watch it now?". That is what we are going to be talking about in this section. When you download a movie or TV show, it will show up in the TV app. This is what the app looks like:

When you first open the app, you will see three tabs at the bottom of your screen:

When you download movies or TV shows, they will show up in the "Library" tab. When you click on the Library tab, you will be met with a screen that looks like this:

As you can see, I have previously downloaded some TV shows and Movies, and you can see that I can view them here. If I click on one of the titles, I can view additional details about them.

For example, if I downloaded a TV show, and I clicked on the title, I would be able to see which season and episode I have downloaded.

When you tap on one of the titles, you will see a screen that looks like this:

In the image above, you can see that I have downloaded episodes seven, eight, and nine of this TV show. When I am ready to watch the episodes, all I have to do is simply tap on the episode the I choose. Then it will start playing.

The other two tabs in the TV app are related to Apple's second streaming service, called Apple TV. We will talk about it in the next section.

ANOTHER STREAMING SERVICE: APPLE TV

There is a second streaming service that Apple offers. It is called Apple TV. It costs $5 per month, and you will have access to hundreds of TV shows and movies that you can watch at any time you would like.

As I mentioned a second go, the last two tabs in the TV app have to do with the Apple TV streaming service.

The "Watch Now" tab is to discover new Apple TV titles that are available for you to watch. Again, these titles are only available to you if you have an Apple TV streaming service subscription.

The other tab, which is "Search", is where you can search for TV Shows or movies that might be included in the Apple TV subscription.

If you have the subscription, and you would like to watch one one of the shows, all you have to do is click the TV show or movie's cover/title.

SIGNING UP FOR APPLE TV

It is super easy to sign up for Apple TV. To do this, you first have to go to the Watch Now tab. If you scroll down a little bit, you might see a section that looks like this:

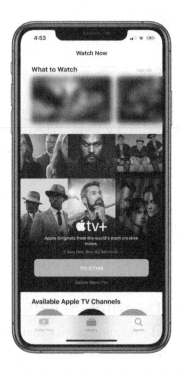

You can tap the "Try It Free" button to begin your seven day trial. Once this seven day trial is over, you will be charged the $5 per month subscription fee.

CHAPTER TWENTY SIX

APPLE PAY

There is this pretty neat feature on your phone that allows you to use your phone like a credit card. Pretty crazy right? It is called Apple Pay, and in this chapter we will learn about what Apple Pay is, how to set it up, and how we can use it in stores.

All of the members in my family use Apple Pay, and it is extremely safe to use! Apple uses some unique technology to ensure that your information is safe on your phone. Something that is quite interesting, is that your credit or debit card number isn't actually stored on your device; instead, there is a unique account number that is created to make sure that your information is completely safe. This also means that the store that you use Apple Pay in won't even get to see your credit/debit card number! It's extra safe!

I mentioned Apple Pay towards the beginning of this book. To sum up what I mentioned earlier, basically Apple Pay is a way of contactless payment, where you simply touch your phone to the Apple Pay receiver at the cash register. This saves you from the steps of getting out your wallet, giving your card, etc. It generally speeds up the process of buying things at the store.

SETTING APPLE PAY UP FOR THE FIRST TIME

Setting up Apple Pay for the first time is actually very simple. To set it up, we first have to open the Wallet app. As the name suggests, this is where you credit or debit card will live. This is what the Wallet app looks like:

When you open the wallet app for the first time, you will see a screen that looks like this:

To add a new credit or debt card, you will have to first press the "+" button in the top right corner. Once you do this, there will be a screen that will give you a little information about what Apple Pay is, and some of the different things that you can use it for. You can press the blue "Continue" button to continue.

On the next screen, you will be given two options:

If you just want to add your current credit or debit card, then you can press the first option, "Credit or Debit Card". The second option, "Apply for Apple Card", is if you would like to apply for Apple's own credit card, the Apple Card.

Typically, you will just want to add your current credit or debit card, so you can just press "Credit or Debit Card".

The next couple of screens will have you to enter in information about your credit/debit card (like the card number, security code, etc).

Once you do that, there will be a screen that asks you to agree to the Terms and Conditions. You can just click the "Agree" button in the bottom right corner.

Depending on the bank that you use, the next screen might ask you to do some sort of Card Verification. For my bank, you have to call them and ask the person on the phone to verify it for you. They might ask for some of your information to verify that it is you. I know that for other banks, they might simply send you a text message with a certain code that you can enter in; it is very case dependent!

Now your card is all ready and set up!

HOW TO USE APPLE PAY IN STORE

When you get to a store, and you want to use Apple Pay, you have to make sure that you see one of these icons near the contactless payment system:

If you see one of these icons, then you're golden, and you can use Apple Pay there. If you aren't sure, you can always ask the cashier and they will be more than happy to let you know!

Even though a lot of stores accept Apple Pay, I would still recommend bring your credit/debit card with you (unless you already know that the store accepts Apple Pay).

When you are at a store and ready to use Apple Pay, you can double press the power button (the one on the right side of your phone), and this screen will come up:

To authenticate, all you have to do is glance at your phone, and Face ID will register your face. If you want to pay with your phone's passcode, you can do that instead (just wait for the Face ID to not be registered, and then you will be prompted to enter in your phone's passcode-the same one you use to unlock your device).

That is the process that you would use if you have Face ID. If you have Touch ID, however, then you can simply rest your finger on the fingerprint sensor, and it will be authenticated.

Once you've used either Face ID or Touch ID (or a passcode) to authenticate, you can hold your phone near the contactless payment reader until you see a checkmark on your screen. Once you see the checkmark, your payment is complete.

> Note: You do not have to unlock your phone first before using Apple Pay to pay for something. You can do it straight from your lock screen.

> Note: To get out of the Apple Pay screen here, you can simply press the power button once, and you will be returned to your lock screen.

You might notice how using Apple Pay is much quicker than paying with a regular debit or credit card. It is a pretty fun experience, to be completely honest, and the cashier will definitely be impressed if you use Apple Pay to checkout! You are now the coolest person in the store!

CHAPTER TWENTY SEVEN

SIRI; YOUR PERSONAL ASSISTANT

By now, you are probably familiar with smart speakers. You know, the little round disks where you can say, "Ok Google," or "Hey Alexa", and they will talk back to you and give you information? What if I told you that your phone could do something very similar.

Already programmed into your phone, there is virtual assistant, called Siri, that can help you use your phone. To access Siri, all you have to do is press and hold the power button. Once you do this, you should see this on your screen:

Here, you can say different commands that Siri will react to. For example, if you say "Text John Hi, Whats up?", Siri will draft a message from you to John, and the message will say "Hi, Whats up?". It will then ask you if you want to send the message, and you can either reply with a "yes" or a "no".

Siri is really smart, and can understand a lot of commands. She is very flexible with the things that you say. If she cannot understand one of your commands or responses, then she will tell you and let you try again.

You can ask Siri to do a ton of things! You can ask her to set alarms, send messages, play music, inform you about the weather, translate words or phrases into different languages, define words, quickly look things up for you, and so much more! You can really play around with Siri! Ask it some things, and see how it responds.

Siri isn't something that I use all the time, but it is pretty fun to play around with. One of the most practical things I can think of for using Siri, is setting timers while you cook. That is what my dad does!

SIRI'S NEW INTERFACE IN IOS 14

In IOS 14, Apple changed the interface of Siri. Instead of covering your whole screen, Siri now pops up along the top or bottom of your screen. It looks something like this:

Whether you have the new IOS 14 Siri interface, or the older Siri interface, Siri works the same, and you will have the same results!

CHAPTER TWENTY EIGHT

THE APP STORE; FIND AN APP THAT WORKS PERFECTLY FOR YOU!

The App Store on your phone allows you to download third-party apps. "Third-party apps", is a term used to describe apps that aren't made by Apple, and so they aren't automatically put on your phone when you first set it up. There are over 2,000,000 apps on the App Store; its pretty crazy!

So. Let's get started and download some apps! This is what the App Store app icon looks like:

When you click on the app icon to open it, you will see five different tabs at the bottom of your screen:

Note: If you see an "Updates" tab instead of an "Arcades" tab, that is totally okay, and we will talk more about this later!

We will go through each tab individually, and explain what each tab does!

THE SEARCH TAB

The first tab that we will talk about, is the search tab. When you tap onto this tab, you will be met with a screen that looks like this:

If you are looking for a specific app, then you can type the name of the app into the search bar. Or, if you are looking for an app with a certain function, you can type it's function in here too. For example, if you are looking for an app that will allow you to play chess, or solitaire, you can type one of those words into the search bar, and once you press search, you will be given search results that are relevant to the thing that you searched.

Side note: I apologize that almost everything is blurred out here; I have to do this so that I can publish this book!

As you can see, various search results pop up. If you see an app you immediately like, you can press the download button. However, if you would like to get more information about an app, you can tap any part of the app listing. Once you do this, this screen will pop up:

When you are on an app listing like this, you can see additional information like screenshots of the app, a description, and even some ratings. This is handy if you want to know if the app you are downloading is good or not. You can even look at some of the screenshots to see what the app looks like, and decide if you like the design of the app or not.

Lastly, if you want to download the app, you can press the download button. The download button can take on various shapes, but they all do the same thing; they will all download the app. But the shape of it can clue you in on some information. I will go into detail about the various types of download buttons, and what they mean:

GET	$3.99	⬇
This means that the app is free to download; it doesn't cost a cent!	If you see a price in the button, then this means that the app costs money, and that you will have to pay to download it.	This means that you've downloaded the app before, and that you can simply re-download it.

In the app store, after you click the download button, you can also see the progress of your download by looking at where the download button used to be. After you click download, it should be replaced by a little timer. This is what it looks like:

You can also watch the app download from your home screen. Exit the App Store app, and on your home screen you should see the app icon, and the same stop-watch icon covering it. You can see how the downloading is progressing by looking at the little stopwatch icon that will cover the app. Once the app has finished downloading you will be able to open it!

This app here is in the process of downloading.

THE "APPS" TAB

The Apps tab, which is the middle tab of the app store, is the tab you can click on to discover new apps that have just been released, recommendations, or just look for additional apps to download. This is kind of like browsing a magazine, but for apps.

You can scroll up and down through all of the categories of apps, and swipe left and right within each category block to look for more apps in that similar category.

If you scroll almost towards the bottom, you will see categories for the "Top Free Apps", and the "Top Paid Apps". You can click the "See All" button to view the long list of the most popular apps right now.

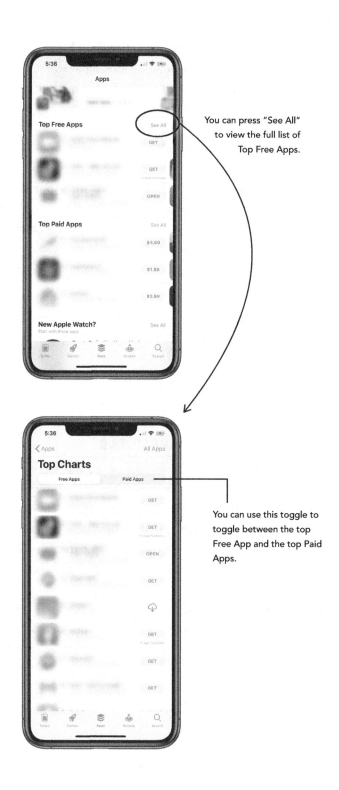

You can press "See All" to view the full list of Top Free Apps.

You can use this toggle to toggle between the top Free App and the top Paid Apps.

Seeing this list is pretty cool, and if you find an app that you are interested in, you can tap the download button to download it.

THE TODAY TAB

The today tab shows little stories or articles that are written about a special app. Sometimes there are stories about how the app was made, or the different features of the app. I don't really use this tab, and you can ignore it unless you'd like to explore it!

THE GAMES TAB

This tab is used to find games that can be played on your phone. These games are usually pretty hard. If you would like to experiment with some pretty serious gaming on your phone, you can explore this tab, but otherwise you can stick to the other ones.

THE ARCADE OR UPDATES TAB

The last tab on your screen will either be titled "Arcade", or it will be titled "Updates"; you will have one or the other. Both of these tabs have completely different functions. The reason that that you can have one or the other, is because in the most recent iOS update, Apple has introduced Apple Arcade. We will talk about this in a second, but they essentially replaced the old "Updates" tab with the new "Arcade" tab.

> Note: If you have iOS 13 or newer, then this fifth tab will be titled "Arcade", and if you have iOS 12 or older, then it will be titled "Updates".

The Arcade tab is to advertise Apple's new App Store streaming service, Apple Arcade. This is similar to how Apple's music streaming service, Apple Music, works. But for Apple Arcade, you pay a monthly price to access a bunch of selected games. The price for Apple Arcade is

$4.99 a month. I don't think I've ever even opened up this tab before.

If you have an older version of iOS software, then you might have the "Updates" tab instead of the Arcade tab. You will use this Updates tab to update your apps. We will talk more about updating your apps in a little bit.

ADDING A CREDIT/DEBIT CARD TO PAY FOR APPS

So, there are two different ways of paying for paid apps (apps that cost money); using a credit/debit card, or using App Store gift cards.

In this section, we will talk about paying with a credit card, and in the next section we will talk about paying with an App Store gift card.

When you were setting up your phone during the set-up process (at the way beginning of this book), you may have chosen to enter in a credit/debit card. If you have already done this, then you are golden!

If you didn't enter your credit/debit card information when you were setting your phone up, then you can do it right now!

To add a credit/debit card, we will first have to go to our Account Settings. First, click the "Account Settings" button in the top right corner. This button will be shown in the top right corner on every tab in the App Store. This is what it looks like:

Once you click this, you will be shown this screen:

To add a credit card, we will have to tap the first button at the very top. It should say your name, and your Apple ID below it. Once you click it, you will be shown this screen:

Once you are here, you can press the "Manage Payments" button.

If you already have a payment method entered in, then it should be shown at the top of your screen. However, if there isn't one there and you would like to add one, then you can click "Add Payment Method". Once you've done this, a form will pop up where you can add your credit/debit card information.

Once everything is entered in, you can click "Done" in the top right corner and everything will be saved.

REDEEMING APP STORE GIFT CARDS

The other way to pay for apps that cost money, is by using App Store gift cards. If you have an App Store gift card, then you can enter it into the App Store app, and use it as money to purchase apps. This is what I do when I want to buy an app that cost money.

If you have an App Store gift card, we will learn how to redeem it right now!

The first thing we have to do, is go to the account settings (if you forget how to do this, reference back to page 284). This is what the account settings page looks like:

If you want to redeem an App Store gift card, you can press "Redeem Gift Card or Code". Once you tap this button, your screen will change to this:

Now you can choose if you would like to enter in the code manually or using the camera.

Note: The code will have to be scratched off on the back side of your gift card to enter it into your phone.

Using the camera on your phone to enter in a gift card code is pretty cool. To use your camera, you can simply tap, "Use Camera". Then, all you have to do is point the back facing camera (the camera viewfinder will pop up on the screen) to the back of the gift card (with the code revealed), and it will automatically register it for you. Then the balance of the gift card will be added to your account. It's that simple!

If you would like to enter in the code manually, you can just tap, "You can also enter your code manually", and you will be prompted to do just that.

UPDATING YOUR APPS

There are two different ways to update apps, and it depends on if you have the Updates tab or the Arcade tab:

METHOD 1: IF YOU HAVE THE UPDATES TAB

If you have iOS 12 or older, then there will be an "Updates" tab at the bottom with the rest of the tabs. This is what the "Updates" icon looks like in your tabs at the bottom of your screen:

If you have the "Updates" tab, and you tap onto it, then you will see this screen:

Once you are here, you can either update each app individually by clicking the "Update" button next to each one of them, or select the

"Update All" button towards the top right of your screen to update them all at once.

METHOD 2: IF YOU HAVE THE ARCADE TAB

If you have iOS 13 or newer, then your apps automatically update for you; there isn't anything that you have to press. However, if you have to manually update them for some reason, or want to check to see if any of your apps need to be manually updated, then you can go to your account settings (if you forget how to access the account settings, you can reference back to page 284).

If you scroll down towards the bottom of the screen (of the account settings), then you will be able to see if there are any apps that need to be updated:

Here, you can either update each individual app individually by clicking the "Update" icon next to each one of them, or select the "Update All" button towards the top left of your screen to update them all at once.

If there are no apps shown here, then this means that all of your apps are up to date!

SOCIAL MEDIA

Using social media is probably one of the most used things on people's phones. Although social media isn't a necessary thing, you might want to look into getting started with it to stay connected to family members, or just simply see what they are up to. Two of the most popular social media apps are Facebook and Instagram. If you are looking to get started in social media, these two apps are probably the best place to start!

CHAPTER TWENTY NINE

THE SETTINGS APP: MAKING YOUR PHONE PERSONAL

Your phone is a very personal device. There are so many different things that you can customize, and a lot of different things that you can do to change the way that your phone looks (both on the outside, and on the inside).

In this chapter, we will talk about how to make your device personal, and change some settings so that it works best for you!

Just about all of the settings on your phone can be found in the Settings app. This is what the Settings app looks like:

When you first open the app, you will be met with a screen that looks like this:

You might already be able to tell that there are so many different options. And you can scroll down, and the list of these options just keeps getting longer and longer. It is pretty crazy, but do not worry one bit! We are going to break down everything in this app, and I will walk you through it all! This will be fun!

Because there are so many different options, I am going to break this chapter up into the different settings that you can change in this app. For example, the first section that we are going to talk about, is changing and connecting to WiFi!

CHANGING/CONNECTING TO WIFI

When you first open the Settings app, you will see a lot of different categories. If you click on one of these categories, they will open up into settings, or in some cases, sub-categories that you can open up further. It is kind of like some type of hierarchy system.

The first category that we are going to explore, is the WiFi category. This is what it looks like:

When you first open this tab, you will see a screen that looks like this:

Here, you can toggle on and off WiFI (you can also do this in the control center), and connect and disconnect to individual WiFi routers. If you want to connect to another WiFi router (maybe you've gone to somebody's house and want to connect to their WiFi), then it will appear in the list under "Networks". Here, if you see a new router name, you can simply tap it. If the router requires a password (which it most likely will), there will be a little pop-up on the screen that asks you to input the password. You can ask the owner of the router what the password is, and they will be able to give it to you.

If you would like to disconnect from a specific WiFi router, you can tap the little "i" icon to the right of the WiFi router's name (there is a little circle with the letter i inscribed in it). Then you can then tap "Forget This Network". This will disconnect you from the network, and if you ever wanted to rejoin the network, you would need to re-enter the password.

Something that is pretty cool about WiFi, is that it will auto-join the WiFi network whenever you are near the router. For example, if you go over the same person's house every Thursday, then your phone will automatically connect to that person's WiFi when you get within the range of their router. This means that you will only have to enter in the WiFi password once!

INCREASING THE VOLUME OF YOUR ALARMS

If you are finding that the volume of your alarm, or the volume of other alert sounds aren't loud enough (or too quiet) on your phone, then you may have to increase (or decrease) the volume of these alerts

Note: These alerts aren't controlled by your regular volume buttons on the side of your phone!

First, we will have to go to the "Sounds and Haptics" category. This is what it looks like:

When you click on this category, you will see this screen:

This is the slider you can slide back and forth to increase or decrease the volume of things like alarms, notifications, etc.

Now you can slide the slider right and left to increase or decrease the volume of these alerts.

You can see other settings here that relate to these types of alerts. You can toggle things like "Vibrate on Ring", which allows you to turn on or off the vibration that happens when your phone rings.

CHANGING THE SOUNDS OF YOUR ALERTS

When your phone is in the Ring Mode, and is making little sounds every time you get a notification, you may or may not like the default sounds that it chooses for you. You are able to change those sounds in settings. If you go into the "Sounds and Haptics" category (just like the section before), you will see a section that is for "Sounds and Vibration Patterns". This is what it looks like:

If you would like to change the sound of the notifications listed on the left, all you have to do is click on the notification category that you would like to change. For example, if I wanted to change the sound of my notifications for text messages, I would click "Text Tone".

Once I click on the notification I wish to change the sound for, I will be able to choose the sound I like from a large list. You can tell which sound you have selected for a certain notification if it has a check mark next to the sound title. You can click through the different sounds until you find one you like.

UPDATING YOUR PHONE

Updating your phone is a relatively simple process. Make sure that you won't need your phone for anything important for the next 45 minutes to an hour, because updating your phone can potentially take a while to do.

If you want to update your phone, the category that you want to click into, is the "General" category. This is what it looks like:

Once you tap into here, you will see additional categories that you can click into if you would like. But, because we want to learn how to update out phones, we will click the "Software Update" button at the top of the screen.

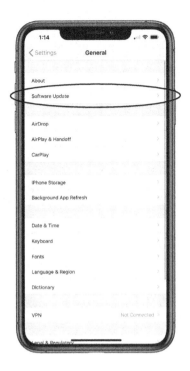

Once you do this, your phone will begin checking for updates. If there is an update available to you, you will see a screen that looks like this:

If you want to proceed with the software update, you can click "Download and Install". The software update will begin downloading.

Make sure that you do not walk away from your phone quite yet. After about 10 minutes of downloading, your phone will require you to verify one more thing before it starts updating.

While your phone is downloading the software update, and updating, I would recommend not using it, as it could slow down the process of updating. Once your phone begins the updating process, your screen will go black, and you will see the glowing apple logo, and a progress bar.

Once your phone is completely finished updating, you will be free to use it again!

> Note: After you update to a newer software, there is no way to go back. In other words, make sure that you are 100% positive that you want to update before you do so.

CUSTOMIZING THE CONTROLS WITHIN CONTROL CENTER

We talked about control center in the beginning of this book. You can add additional controls to your control center, like quick access to alarms, text size, voice memos, and more. To do this, we will click on the "Control Center" category in the settings app. It looks like this:

 Control Center

Once you click on it, you will see a screen that looks like this:

Once you are here, you can click on "Customize Controls". Then you will see a screen that looks like this:

Here is where you can add (or take away) controls to your control center. If you want to add a certain control to your control center, you can click the green "+" button that is to the left of the control title. If you want to take away any controls, you can click the red "-" button. At any point, you can pull down on the top right corner to access control center to view what your new, updated, and personalized control center looks like!

CHANGING TEXT SIZE

Changing text size is something that you should probably play with so that your device is easy to read. If you want to change your text size, first we will have to click on the category labeled "Display and Brightness". This is what it looks like:

Once you open this tab, you will be met with a screen that looks like this:

To change text size, you can click the "Text Size" button towards the bottom. Once you do this, you will see a screen that looks like this:

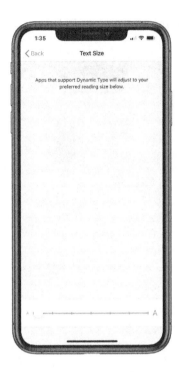

At the bottom of the screen, you can see a slider where you can adjust your text size. The more you slide it to the right, the larger the text, and visa versa. You can see a piece of sample text at the top of your screen to see what the text size that you selected will look like.

HOW TO GET EXTRA-EXTRA BIG TEXT SIZES

If you are finding that you are at the largest text size, and it just still isn't big enough for you, well you are in luck! There is a solution to this problem; an extra-large text size toggle.

To access this, we will first go to the "Accessibility" category (for some reason, this extra-large text she toggle is in a completely different category). This is what it looks like:

Once you click into this category, you will see a ton of other sub-categories. The sub-category that we are looking for, is called "Display & Text Size". Once you click into this screen, you will be shown a multitude of different options:

Next, tap on the "Larger Text" button. It is the second button from the top.

Once you tap this button, your screen should look like this:

Now, you can press the "Large Accessibility Sizes" toggle at the top of your screen, and at the bottom of your screen, you will see that the text size can now get much much larger.

CHANGING YOUR WALLPAPER!

Changing your wallpaper is one of the ways that you can truly change the way that your device looks. To change your wallpaper, you can click on the category titled "Wallpaper".

Once you click on that, your screen should look like this:

If you want to set a new wallpaper, you can click "Choose a New Wallpaper". Once you do this, you will be given two options; you can either select a wallpaper from Apple's default wallpapers, or create a wallpaper from one of your own photos. If you select a wallpaper from your photos, you can really make your phone personal. Maybe you can set it to a picture of your family, or your children/grandchildren!

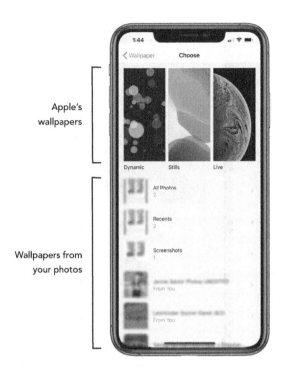

Apple's wallpapers

Wallpapers from your photos

Regardless of wether you want one of Apple's wallpapers, or one of your own, you can open the albums of photos by just tapping on them. Once you do this, the album will expand, and you will be given multiple different options for images that you can set as your background.

When you select a picture that you want as your wallpaper, you can click on it to see what it would look like as your lockscreen.

If you don't like the way it looks, you can click "Cancel". If you like the way that it looks, you can click "Set". This will bring up these three options:

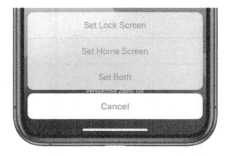

If you set the image as your lock screen, it will only show up on your lock screen. If you set the image as your home screen, it will only show up on your home screen (where all of your app icons are). You can also "Set Both", where it will set the image as your lockscreen and home screen. Yay! Now your wallpaper is set! You can exit out of the Settings app to admire your wonderful new lockscreen or new home screen! Isn't it crazy how drastic it changes the way your phone looks?

CHANGING YOUR PHONE'S PASSCODE

Sometimes you might want to change your phone's passcode. If you want to do this, you will first have to open the "Face ID & Passcode" category. It looks like this:

Note: This category could be named something else if you have Touch ID.

Once you click into this category, you will have to enter your phone's passcode. Once the passcode is entered in completely, you will see this screen:

If you scroll down a little bit, you will see these options:

If you click "Change Passcode", you will first have to enter in your old passcode again, and then your new passcode. It will ask you to type your new passcode once more (for a total of two times). Now your new passcode is set!

DEACTIVATING AUTO-BRIGHTNESS

We talked a little bit about auto brightness when we were talking about the control center. Auto brightness is when your phone will adjust your brightness automatically to adapt to the conditions of your environment. For example, if you walk outside, your brightness will go up. If you walk indoors, or into a dark room, your brightness will go down.

Sometimes this is pretty cool, but sometimes it can be a little annoying; especially if like your phone's screen to be bright.

In this section, we will learn how to turn this feature off so that your brightness level will remain constant!

To do this, we will first go to the "Accessibility" category. This is what it looks like:

Once you click into this category, you will see a ton of other sub-categories. The sub-category that we are looking for, is called "Display & Text Size". Once you click into this category, you will be shown a multitude of different options. If you scroll down all the way to the bottom, you will see the "Auto-Brightness" toggle:

You can switch that bottom toggle off, and now auto-brightness will be turned off!

A TRICK IF YOU ARE STUCK...

Due to the fact that there are so many settings in this app, it can be quite difficult to go through them all and look for a certain setting if you don't really know where to look. Luckily, most of the categories and sub-categories in the Settings app are labeled pretty well, and sometimes you can find your way through them. But sometimes, you just can't find a setting you are looking for.

If you find yourself in this situation, you can always default to the search bar at the top of the list of categories (scroll all the way to the top of the list of categories).

Here, you can type in the specific setting you are looking for, and there should be a couple of search results that pop up. If you find what you are looking for in the search results, you can simply press on one of them, and it will automatically jump to the place where you can find the toggle or option to change the setting that you are looking for!

WRAPPING UP THE CHAPTER

Congratulations! You've finished a really complex and hard to understand section of this book. I think the sheer number of settings within this app are kind of intimidating, if I am being honest.

The only way to really learn about what all these settings do, is by going through the lists themselves and reading all of the options. This is how I learned what each of the different settings do.

CHAPTER THIRTY

EDITING YOUR HOME SCREEN APP LAYOUT & DELETING APPS

When you first set up your phone, your apps are organized in the default app layout. However, there is a way to change the layout of the apps, and which apps you want where on the page. In this chapter, we will talk about rearranging apps, and how you can further customize the app layout on your home screen!

Before we begin, though, there is something that I have to mention. In iOS 14, Apple completely changed the way that you edit, organize, and delete the apps on your home screen. So, I am going to split this chapter into two sections. Section One will be for people that have iOS 13 or earlier, and Section Two will be for people that have iOS 14 or later.

SECTION 1: iOS 13 OR BEFORE

If you would like to edit your home screen, you first have to enter the "Wiggle Mode". To enter wiggle mode, you have to press and hold on an app (it can be any app), and you will see these options pop up underneath the app. Once these options pop up, you can release your finger from the screen:

Note: Depending on the app that you choose to press-and-hold on, you might get additional options that pop up in addition to the two options shown in the image above (for example, if you press-and-hold on the Messages app, you might get the option to create a New Message). If this is the case, do not worry; they are just additional "shortcuts" that the app has. For simplicity sake, we can just ignore the other options that show up.

What you can do now, is press "Edit Home Screen", and the apps will start to wiggle. This is where the name wiggle-mode comes from!

If you would like to rearrange apps, all you have to do is drag them around (when they are wiggling).

In this picture, I am showing the process of customizing your home screen. After I long-pressed on an icon, and selected, "Edit Home Screen", the apps started to wiggle (and you can see the "X" in every corner of the apps). I wanted to move the Podcast app towards the top of the phone, so I placed my finger on the app icon, and dragged it upwards. As you do this, you will see that the apps around your finger will part and fill in around the app that you are holding underneath your finger. When I find the place I want to put the app, I can simply lift up my finger.

When you are done, and you want to exit the wiggle-mode, you can simple click the "Done" button in the top right corner. This will make the apps stop wiggling, and you can resume using your phone normally.

Note: If you would like to move an app to another page on your phone, you can simply place your finger on the app (when it is wiggling), and drag it towards the very side of the phone (like the right side of the phone if you want to move the app one page to the right). After a couple of seconds, the page will slide over, and you will be on the next page. If you change your mind and would like to bring your app back to the page that it was previously on, you can simply drag the app back to the other side of the phone, and after a couple of seconds, you will be back to the original page. Then you can release the app, and it will fall back with the rest of the apps.

You might also notice that there will be a gray "X" in the top left corner of every app (look at the picture on the previous page for reference). If you wanted to delete an app, you can press this "X". If you do press it, then you will get a last-minute alert asking if you are sure you want to delete the app. If you click "Delete", the app will be deleted.

> Tip: You may also notice how when you long press on an app icon, there is also a "Delete App" option (look at the image on page 318). You can press the "Delete App"option shown here if you wish to delete an app, in addition to the method that was described in the last paragraph.

SECTION 2: iOS 14 OR LATER

If you have iOS 14 or newer installed on your phone, then this section is for you!

If you would like to edit your home screen, you first have to enter the "Wiggle Mode". To enter wiggle mode, you have to press and hold on an app (it can be any app), and you will see these options pop up underneath the app. Once these options pop up, you can release your finger from the screen:

> Note: Depending on the app that you choose to press-and-hold on, you might get additional options that pop up in addition to the two options shown in the image above (for example, if you press-and-hold on the Messages app, you might get the option to create a New Message). If this is the case, do not worry; they are just additional "shortcuts" that the app has. For simplicity sake, we can just ignore the other options

that show up.

What you can do now, is press "Edit Home Screen", and the apps will start to wiggle. This is where the name wiggle-mode comes from!

If you would like to rearrange apps, all you have to do is drag them around (when they are wiggling).

In this picture, I am showing the process of customizing your home screen. After I long-pressed on an icon, and selected, "Edit Home Screen", the apps started to wiggle (and you can see the "X" in every corner of the apps). I wanted to move the Podcast app towards the top of the phone, so I placed my finger on the app icon, and dragged it upwards. As you do this, you will see that the apps around your finger will part and fill in around the app that you are holding underneath your finger. When I find the place I want to put the app, I can simply lift up my finger.

When you are done, and you want to exit the wiggle-mode, you can simple click the "Done" button in the top right corner. This will make the apps stop wiggling, and you can resume using your phone normally.

Note: If you would like to move an app to another page on your phone, you can simply place your finger on the app (when it is wiggling), and drag it towards the very side of the phone (like the right side of the phone if you want to move the app one page to the right).

After a couple of seconds, the page will slide over, and you will be on the next page. If you change your mind and would like to bring your app back to the page that it was previously on, you can simply drag the app back to the other side of the phone, and after a couple of seconds, you will be back to the original page. Then you can release the app, and it will fall back with the rest of the apps.

You might also notice that there will be a gray "-" in the top left corner of every app. If you wanted to delete an app, you can press this "-". Once you do press it, you will be given three options; to delete the app, move the app to the App Library, or to cancel:

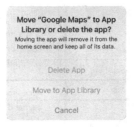

If you wanted to delete the app, then you can simply press "Delete App". It will ask you if you are sure, and if you are, you can click "Delete".

Tip: You may also notice how when you long press on an app icon, there is also a "Delete App" option. (look at the image on page 320). You can press the "Delete App"option shown here if you wish to delete an app, in addition to the method that was described in the last paragraph. This method is a little bit simpler and easier to remember.

Now, lets briefly talk about the "Move to App Library" option (look at the image on the previous page). You may remember me talking about the App Library in Chapter Ten. Essentially, the App Library is where you can view all of the apps that you have downloaded onto your phone. What the "Move to App Library" button does, is it removes the app from your home screen, and puts it into the App Library. This means that the app isn't necessarily deleted from your phone, but just simply not shown on your home screen. There are very few cases where someone would actually do this, but if you want to experiment with hiding apps from your home screen, you are now able to do it.

The last thing that we are going to talk about with regards to customizing your home screen on your phone, is how to add widgets to your home screen. This is what they look like:

As you can see in the picture, Widgets are nice because they give you access to quick pieces of information from various apps. In the image above, I have two widgets; one Weather app widget, and one Calendar app widget. In the Weather app widget, you can see things like temperature, weather conditions, etc. In the Calendar app widget, you can see things like upcoming events, and today's date.

There are three different types of widgets; small, medium, and large sizes. The small widgets take up a 2-by-2 grid on your home screen. An example of this, is the Weather app widget that I have in the image on the previous page.

> Note: When I say "a 2-by-2 grid", I am talking about the grid that the app icons make on your home screen. The small widget size takes up a 2-by-2 grid, which means that the length of this widget is 2 app icons, and the width of this widget is 2 app icons.

The medium-sized widgets, take up a 4-by-2 grid on your phone's screen. An example of this, would be the Calendar app widget that is shown on the previous page. The large-sized widgets are absolutely massive; they take up a 4-by-4 grid on your phone's screen.

To add a widget to your home screen, you first have to enter wiggle-mode (if you forget how to do this, reference back to page 320). Now that you are in wiggle-mode, do you see the "+" button in the very top left corner of your screen? This is the button that you are going to press if you would like to add a widget to your home screen.

Once you do that, a screen will slide up from the bottom, and you will be shown various suggested widgets that you are able to add to your home screen. If you scroll down to the bottom of this screen, you will see a list of various apps. These apps (like Batteries, Calendar, Clock, etc.) are apps in which you can create your own widget for, and set the size that you would like the widget to be (small, medium, or large). When you find a widget that you are pleased with, you can simply click the "+ Add Widget" button that is at the very bottom of your screen, and the widget will be added to your home screen. Its that easy!

> Note: If you wanted to delete a widget from your home screen, you can use the same process that you use for

deleting a regular app; first hold down the widget you wish to delete, then once the options pop up, you can press "Edit Home Screen", and you will enter wiggle-mode. Once in wiggle-mode, you can click the "-" in the top left corner of the specific widget you wish to delete, and then click "Remove". Its that simple!

CREATING FOLDERS FOR APPS

This last section applies to everyone, regardless of the iOS version that you have installed on your phone. In this section, we are going to talk about how to create folders for your apps.

Creating folders for your apps is very simple. To create a folder, you first have to enter wiggle-mode. Once you do this, you can simply drag one app, and hold it over another app. After a couple of seconds, a folder will open up, and the two apps will be placed inside of the folder you just created.

If you would like to rename the folder, you can simply tap on the name of the folder, just above the gray square where the apps will sit. Once you are done looking inside of this folder, you can simply tap below the gray square where the apps will sit, and you will be back at your home screen.

If you would like to add another app to the folder, all you have to do is take another app off of the home screen, drag it over the folder you just created, and the app will jump inside, just like the others.

If you want to bring an app back outside of a folder, and back onto the home screen, all you have to do is pick up the app (while it is wiggling), and drag it outside of the gray square where all of the apps in the folder sit. After holding the app outside of the folder for a couple of seconds, you will be back at the home screen, and you can place the app wherever you would like to!

Yay! Hopefully now your home screen's layout is the way that you like it! It is fun to rearrange the apps on your phone, and makes your phone look like it is truly yours!

CHAPTER THIRTY ONE

YOU ARE AMAZING!

CONGRATULATIONS! WOOHOO! I am so unbelievably proud of you! You've accomplished so much!

It is crazy how far you've come in your journey through this book. At the start of this book, you knew very little about your phone. Now you know how to do a whole bunch of stuff!

I planned out the order of how I would teach you the things in this book based on a couple of factors. First, I wanted to make sure that you knew how to do all of the basic things (like calling, texting, unlocking your phone) at the beginning of the book. As we got further and further into the book, the intensity of the content definitely ramped up! Some of the things that we talked about in this book are pretty advanced things when you think about it!

When we began our journey through this book, I wanted you to challenged yourself; you know, really try and learn how to use your phone. You've definitely challenged yourself reading this book. And because of that, you've also accomplished so much!

I cannot keep saying how proud I am of you! You are amazing; don't ever forget that!

I would also like to thank you! Thank you for joining me on this journey. Thank you for letting <u>me</u> teach you about your phone. I had an absolute blast with you, and I hope that you had fun too!

Before we go our own separate ways, I would like to challenge you. I challenge you to keep on learning. Keep on learning about new ways to do things on your phone. Keep on discovering what all of the small buttons and other settings are on your phone. Keep on learning about how to download fun apps and games. I have given you the foundation of how to use your phone. But it is up to you to build the rest of the house and explore it for yourself.

There is one last thing; before you get up from reading this book, I want you to FaceTime a family member or friend. Share amazing memories with those you love and those who you surround yourself with. I can remember the way that I felt when my grandmother FaceTimed me for the first time. We were both filled with so much joy!

Thank you so much again, and I look forward to "seeing" you in the future! I had a blast with you! :)

ABOUT THE AUTHOR

From Science and Technology to English and the Arts, Carter Kowalski has a lot of different interests.

Growing up exclusively in the twenty-first century has allowed him to have a unique perspective when writing this book, as he has used technology, especially Apple devices, for his entire life. Carter has also taken the time to learn how technology works, and how it shapes our lives today.

From helping his grandparents, to helping friends or other family members, Carter has become the "go-to-guy" for solving problems with technological devices.

This is Carter's first piece of literary work, but suspects that it will not be has last! If you would like to follow along his journey, you can visit his website:

https://authorcarterkowalski.wixsite.com/books

Carter Kowalski

Made in the USA
Middletown, DE
23 January 2021

32283415R00195